TRANSITION MAGICIAN

FOR FAMILIES

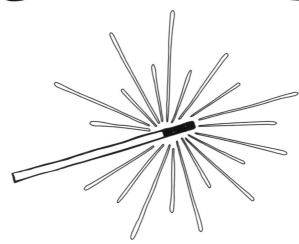

Helping Parents and Children with Everyday Routines

by Ruth Chvojicek, Mary Henthorne, and Nola Larson
Illustrated by Mary Henthorne

Redleaf Press
a division of Resources for Child Caring

Published by: Redleaf Press
                  a division of Resources for Child Caring
                  450 N. Syndicate, Suite 5
                  St. Paul, MN 55104

Distributed by: Gryphon House
                  Mailing Address:
                  P.O. Box 207
                  Beltsville, MD 20704-0207

Library of Congress Cataloging-in-Publication Data

Chvojicek, Ruth, 1956-
    Transition magician for families : helping parents and children with
    everyday routines / by Ruth Chvojicek, Mary Henthorne, and
    Nola Larson.
            p. cm.
    Includes bibliographical references.
    ISBN 1-929610-02-5 (pbk.)
     1. Child rearing. 2. Preschool children. 3. Creative activities and seat
    work. 4. Early childhood education—Parent participation. 5. Home
    and school. 6. Parenting—Study and teaching. I. Henthorne, Mary,
    1952- II. Larson, Nola, 1941- III. Title.

HQ769 .C569 2001
649' .1—dc21

00-068846

In the busy, stressful times of raising young children, this book is dedicated to the children. May their lives be filled with a little more fun and magic!

Acknowledgments

A special thank you to our husbands, Ken, Jeff, and John, for their patience and support while we worked on this project. Thank you to Ruth's children, Jennifer and Benjamin Chvojicek, who provided the wonderful memories that were the inspiration behind writing this book for parents.

Thank you to our friends and colleagues and to early childhood professionals, who have been receptive to our ideas and who have encouraged our work.

Thank you to our QNET colleague, Kathy Boisvert, for her Pizza Box Felt Board idea, and to a Head Start colleague from afar, Kathryn Bell, for her Love Tickets idea.

And finally, thank you to our editor at Redleaf Press, Beth Wallace, for her thoughtful and gentle guidance in helping us work through our thoughts and ideas for *Transition Magician for Families*.

Contents

Introduction

Susan and her three-year-old son Michael had been in the waiting room of the doctor's office for almost thirty minutes. Michael, well past being able to sit quietly and look at books, crawled underneath the chairs across from Susan. An elderly couple across the waiting room gave Susan looks that made her feel like she was a terrible parent. Susan was at her wits' end. She had picked Michael up from day care and driven forty-five minutes to the doctor, and now they were sitting and waiting again. She knew they would have to wait still more inside the exam room, and then there was the forty-five-minute car ride home again. She wished she had remembered to bring some toys along for Michael to play with, but he quickly tired of all his familiar toys from home, anyway. There had to be an easier way to help Michael get through these times.

A child's day is full of transitions. There are transitions outside the home—for example, traveling from home to preschool or day care, from one child care program to another, trips in the car. There are waits at the grocery store, Laundromat, doctor's office, and siblings' sporting events. Children also have to make transitions at home—preparing to leave the house in the morning, getting ready for bed, waiting for a meal, picking up toys, and so on. Changing focus to move from one activity to the next is hard enough for adults, who feel some degree of control over their daily schedules. It can be very difficult for young children, to whom schedule changes often seem random. It's hard on adults to wait for long periods of time, and nearly impossible for young children.

Caregivers know that a child needs quality time with a parent in order to grow up healthy, happy, and secure, and yet parents and children are increasingly busy with activities outside the home, and increasingly occupied by the many tasks of running a household when they are home. Children today have many transitions to manage in a day, and less attention and time than ever from the adults in their lives. Professional caregivers can use this book to help parents turn those precious minutes with their children into quality family time.

As we wrote this book, we kept in mind all the families struggling with the everyday situations described above. In workshops on our previous books for teachers, *Transition Magician* and *Transition Magician 2*, parents have described their challenges in guiding their children through everyday transitions and routines. In *Transition Magician for Families*, we have written activities for parents and children to do both at home and away from home, not just to survive transition times but to enjoy and make the most of these valuable opportunities for building skills and relationships. We have adapted many ideas for use at home from both *Transition Magician* and *Transition Magician 2*, and added fun new ideas as well. All the activities either can be done without special materials, or use props that can be made easily and inexpensively at home with the instructions given here.

While this book has ideas for parents, it is actually written for early childhood professionals to use in their work of supporting the parents of young children. In the first chapter of the book, we discuss the ways that early childhood professionals can support parents to help their children manage transitions. The next five chapters present a collection of activities to use during everyday transition times. The activities are divided into five categories according to the type of transition time they might be used in and children's developmental needs during transition times. The five transition categories are:

* **Everyday Routines**—activities to help a parent guide a child smoothly through routines at home, such as leaving the house in the morning, picking up toys, or getting ready for bed.

* **Busy Times**—activities for a child to do on his or her own while the parent is busy with household routines and responsibilities, such as preparing the meal, talking on the telephone, cleaning the house, or studying.

* **Together Times**—quality activities for parent and child to do together when they are in between the routines of the day.

* **On the Move**—activities for children to do while traveling, both on the everyday trip to school or child care, and on longer trips.

* **While You Wait**—activities to do while waiting at places away from home such as the doctor's office or laundry, or in quiet places such as religious services.

All the activities are written in a reproducible form so that they may be photocopied and given to parents.

The final chapter shows early childhood professionals how to design and set up two *Transition Magician* workshops (one for parents, the other for parents and children) using the transition ideas and props from this book.

We hope that the ideas in this book will be useful for early childhood professionals in supporting the families they work with. Children grow up so quickly. Parents can do more than just "get through" the hectic busy days of raising children, and people who work in early childhood can help them. The ideas in this book will help you to support parents so that they can cherish every opportunity they have to create memories of fun, special activities with their children each day.

Helping Parents with Transitions

On a daily basis, early childhood professionals interact with parents about the struggles parents encounter in handling their everyday routines and transitions. The job of early childhood professionals is not only to help children grow and learn but also to help parents learn about their children and grow together as a healthy family.

Here are some ways you can support parents in handling routines and transitions:

★ Become an expert on child development. Often the behavior that parents struggle with is normal behavior for a child of that age, and it's the parents who have to change their expectations or behavior—not the child. Be prepared to share your expert knowledge with parents. Tell them it's the child's "job" to do things such as explore and run so that muscles stretch and grow properly. Provide written information on normal child development at different ages. At the same time, it's crucial to be sensitive to cultural differences in expectations of children. You may need to adapt the information you give parents to their cultural backgrounds and expectations.

★ If the children and families in your classroom are made up of a diverse group of cultures and backgrounds, spend some time finding out about appropriate expectations for each one. The best way to do this is to talk with the parents. Ask questions such as "Tell me what it was like growing up in your family as a young child," or "Are things different for your child growing up today than they were for you when you were a child? If so, how?"

★ Read and learn more about the development of a child's brain. Current research emphasizes that quality parent-child interactions are vital to the child's healthy growth and development. Research also shows us that both the stress in a child's life and exposure to television can impede the growth of the brain. It is important for all early childhood professionals to know this information and share it with parents and also to share activities that support the healthy growth of the brain. Appendix A recommends books on brain development.

* Become familiar with the Parent Pointer activity pages in this book. They are intended to be photocopied and handed out to parents. Many of the ideas require no props. When a parent approaches you with a specific problem, be prepared to suggest a specific activity or two that might help.

* Prepare a selection of props to lend or give to parents.

* At conference time, make copies of the Parent Pointers to hand out if the topic of routines and transitions comes up in the conversation. Keep a sample prop on hand to show to the parent and the child. The majority of the props are made with inexpensive materials found around the house. Seeing the colorful, easy-to-make props could motivate parents to try the activities with their children.

* If your center or agency has the resources, you might consider developing transition kits for the parents to borrow. A transition kit might include several Parent Pointer sheets and the accompanying props. For example, the Dinnertime Box might include activities for a child to do while the parent is cooking dinner (see Busy Times), or the Traveling Box might include activities for a child to do while traveling (see On the Move activities). Parents would check out these transition kits to use at home. Use an in-service day or take a day before your program year opens to bring teachers and parent volunteers together to assemble the kits.

* Make a special area on your parent bulletin board for a "Transition Tip of the Week." Include the handout "Tips for Parents" (see appendix C), which gives general guidelines for handling routines and transitions. Each month you might feature a different routine or transition time, such as bedtime, leaving the house in the morning, or waiting in the doctor's office. Display samples of the props that are designed for those times, along with photocopies of the Parent Pointers that go with them.

* If your center or agency has a regular newsletter for families, photocopy the Parent Pointers, one or two at a time, and attach them to the newsletter. You might even take a photo of a parent and child doing an activity or using a prop to place in the newsletter alongside the Parent Pointer.

* Sponsor a transition workshop for parents. Early childhood professionals and parents can share resources and ideas that have worked for them. Workshops are a wonderful way to get parents involved in your early childhood program. A good place to start is to conduct an informal survey of your parents to find out which routines and transitions are bothering them the most. Parents have very busy schedules, so it's important to plan something that will be motivating and exciting for them.

Chapter 7 outlines two workshops that could be offered at any early childhood program, and of course they can be adapted to meet the specific needs of your program.

* Photocopy the "Tips for Parents" handout in appendix C, and give it to parents who seem to be struggling with transitions in their children's lives.

2 Everyday Routines

Activities to help parents guide children smoothly through routines at home.

Normal daily routines are often challenging for families. It is common to have parents rush in the door of the child care center fretting about the early morning rush out of the house, or complaining that their child "just wouldn't get ready in the morning." This time can be so difficult that many children arrive at school either with breakfast in hand or without breakfast at all. Parents often ask for ideas about how to handle bedtime and toy cleanup, two other commonly troublesome times. The activities in this chapter are written just for these times. They will help parents and children prepare for everyday routines, get through them with less stress, and actually have fun along the way.

Beat the Clock

When cleanup time becomes tedious and difficult for your child, set a timer. Children love to play "beat the clock." Setting a timer for children to race at cleanup time will spur them to move quickly to get those toys picked up. Choose either a bell-type kitchen timer or an hourglass timer that must be watched rather than listened for.

Start by setting guidelines with your child, to encourage putting toys away with care. Set the timer for a realistic amount of time (for example, eight to ten minutes to start with) so that your child can experience success. As your child gets faster, you can gradually cut back on the number of minutes. As with any strategy you try with your child, put the timer away when he or she tires of it and get it out again a few months later.

You can also use the timer to help children get dressed quickly in the morning, or to get ready for bed.

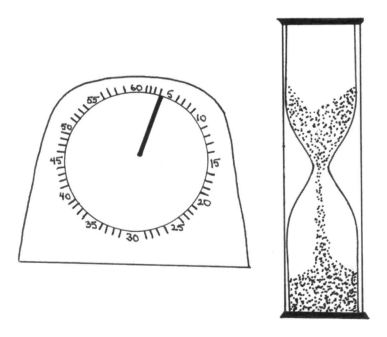

Job and Joy Jars

There are many jobs around the house with which children can help. For example, they can help clean out drawers and toy chests, sweep the floor, rake leaves and weed gardens, or wipe down cupboards and appliances.

Make a list of tasks that don't need to be done daily or weekly. Write each of them on a separate piece of paper. Then, think of enjoyable activities to do with your child (consult him or her for specific ideas) and write these on separate pieces of paper. Some activities might include going for a bike ride, to a movie, or to the park for a picnic.

Write *Jobs* on one jar and *Joys* on the other and place the pieces of paper in the jars. When you have some free time such as a Saturday morning, have your child pick one paper from each jar. Work together to get your "job" done, then make a plan for your "joy" activity. It should be on the same day or in the very near future.

©2001 *Transition Magician for Families*; Redleaf Press, 450 North Syndicate, Suite 5, St. Paul, MN 55104, 800-423-8309

Parent Pointer
BUSY TIMES

Let Me Hand It to You

If you have difficulty getting your child to "give you a hand" with simple responsibilities around the house, try using "hand" tickets. Give your child a ticket whenever he or she carries out a requested task. Keep track of the tickets on a hand-shaped poster. Decide ahead of time how many tickets your child needs to accumulate in order to choose a special activity to do with you.

Materials:
Poster board
Hand-shaped stickers
Self-adhesive Velcro strip, approximately
  six inches
Clear Con-Tact paper

Directions:
1. To make the poster, use a felt-tipped marker to trace your hand onto poster board. Leave about an inch between your hand and the marker, so that the poster ends up slightly larger than your hand. If you wish, write *Let Me Hand It to You* in the center of the hand.

2. Cut out the hand shape and cover it with Con-Tact paper.

3. Cut the strip of Velcro into pieces approximately one-quarter inch long. Attach the hooked side of the Velcro pieces to the poster, spacing the pieces evenly around the hand.

4. To make the tickets, stick the hand-shaped stickers onto another piece of poster board, leaving about two inches between stickers. Draw a small circle around each sticker. Cover the poster board with Con-Tact paper and cut out the circles. Make at least as many tickets as your child needs to collect to gain her reward.

5. Attach a looped piece of Velcro to the back of each ticket.

Lights Out

We show respect to children when we give them time to wind up what they are doing or to make a plan to save it for another time, rather than suddenly telling them it is time to pick up their toys. Children also cooperate better when they have some warning!

Dimming or turning off lights can be a cue to your child that it will soon be time to pick up toys. Approximately five minutes before your child is to begin picking up, dim the lights or turn them off briefly, and calmly announce that in a few minutes it will be time to pick up toys. After five minutes have passed, dim the lights again and announce that it is now time to pick up toys.

Using this signal consistently gives children a sense of security and makes it easier for them to do what you expect them to do.

Magic Pickup Lotion

Cleanup time is a challenging time for many parents. Make it a little "magical" for your child by introducing "magic pickup lotion." Just rub a little glitter lotion on his or her hands, and your child will pick up a roomful of toys in no time at all. You could have even more fun by rubbing a little lotion on your hands first. Make your hands start to quiver and shake, then zoom into picking up toys. As with any strategy you try with your child, when the novelty wears off, put it away for a while. Reintroduce it at a later time.

Materials:
Small plastic bottle (such as a lotion bottle from your stay at a motel)
Baby lotion
Glitter
Sticker to label the bottle

Directions:
1. Fill a small plastic bottle with baby lotion.
2. Add a small pinch of glitter and shake the bottle.
3. Add a label that reads *Magic Pickup Lotion*.

Note: Use a mild lotion and be aware that your child might be sensitive to perfumes.

Magnificent Massages

People of all ages can enjoy a massage. Research also shows that massages are healthy for you both physically and mentally. Take some time to massage your child. He or she may even reciprocate by giving you one.

Massages can be done any time of the day, but they are especially effective at night or first thing in the morning. Tenderly rub your child's back, arms, and face as he or she drifts off to sleep. Hum or sing quietly.

A massage on shoulders, legs, and toes makes a pleasant wake-up call for your child. Quietly talk to him or her about the day's events and the joys that are to come. Starting the day off on a good note can make all the difference in the world for your relationship with your child. Ending a busy day with positive feelings is sure to bring sweet dreams.

Mini Picture Album

Help your child adjust to being away from you while at child care or preschool with a mini picture album that you make just for him or her.

When developing photos, have doubles made. Put the extras in a small, inexpensive photo holder, glue them into a small notebook, or simply place them in a box. Whenever your child is feeling lonely, he or she can pull out pictures of the family, home, pet, or even favorite toys. It will be a wonderful comfort for your child.

For a fun variation of this, take some photos of your child doing exercises such as hopping on one foot, touching toes, twirling arms, or doing jumping jacks. Children enjoy looking at pictures of themselves and will be motivated to try these exercises again when they see the photos.

Nonsense Statements

Have you ever gone to pick up your child from the child care center, and found the child so busy playing that he or she doesn't want to leave with you? You can help to relieve the stress of the moment with a nonsense statement such as, "When we get home we'll need to take the elephant for a walk," or "Come on, we have to get going to catch the space shuttle home." As you laugh together, your child will forget about wanting to play longer and will get ready to go home with no tears.

Pictorial Schedule

Young children have a hard time understanding the passage of time. Sometimes this makes it difficult for children to wait for something to happen (such as waiting for you to pick them up at the end of the day). Try making a Pictorial Schedule of your child's day. You can review it at the beginning of the day with your child so that there is something concrete to look at that will remind him or her of the things that happen throughout the day.

As each event takes place, the child can turn the card over to keep track of where he or she is in the day's activities. Another option is to make a schedule of a specific portion of the day that might be difficult for your child, such as early morning. For example, first place a picture of getting dressed, then a picture of eating breakfast, then brushing teeth, and so on. The picture cards are placed on a Velcro strip so that you can change the order of the activities if needed and turn the cards over as routines are completed.

Materials:

White poster board

Pictures of routines, activities, and transitions typically found in your day; use actual photos of your children, or drawings, or magazine illustrations

Adhesive-backed Velcro strip, ½ yard by ½ inch wide

Marker

Directions:

1. Cut poster board into 4-by-9-inch pieces—one per routine, transition, or activity.
2. Glue pictures to the poster-board pieces (one picture per card) and label each (for example, brushing teeth, arriving at child care).
3. Attach the hooked half of the Velcro strip in a vertical or horizontal line on the wall.
4. Attach a 1-by-1-inch strip of looped Velcro on the back of each card and a second piece on the front, above the illustration, so that the card can be turned over.

Parent Pointer
EVERYDAY ROUTINES

Point the Way

Do you need a little help getting your child to pick up toys? Have some fun by using this "hand wand" with your child at cleanup time. Made from an inexpensive stretchy knit glove, this wand will grab your child's attention and help you give the message to clean. Simply point to the items that need to be picked up, and then point to where you want them to go. The fingers on the wand fold over, so you can use it to indicate the number of things you want your child to pick up, too. You can also take turns with your child, and give him or her the wand to point!

Materials:
Stretchy glove (one-size-fits-all)
Polyester fiberfill
¼-inch dowel (9 inches long) or chop-
  stick
Sandpaper
Fabric glue, or hot glue gun
5 small pieces of Velcro, hooked half only

Directions:
1. Sand the dowel to make it smooth on one end. (If you use a chopstick you can omit this step.)
2. Stuff the glove sparingly with fiberfill, enough to give it form, but loosely enough so that the fingers can still bend easily.
3. Cover 1 inch of one end of the dowel with glue and insert it approximately 2 inches into the stuffing in the glove.
4. Squeeze the stuffing around the stick to secure it.
5. Glue the opening of the glove closed around the stick.
6. Glue a small piece of the hooked Velcro to the tip of each finger. The hooks of the Velcro will stick to the loops in the knitted glove. This allows you to bend the fingers down so that the hand can point or indicate the number of things you want your child to pick up.

©2001 *Transition Magician for Families*; Redleaf Press, 450 North Syndicate, Suite 5, St. Paul, MN 55104, 800-423-8309

Puppet Patrol

Using puppets is a great way to get children to do tasks. There is something magical about puppets—children respond to them more readily than to the familiar voice of a parent. Make a simple puppet (or several) with your child and have it remind your child of morning tasks such as dressing, washing, and brushing teeth. Puppets can also chat with a child who is sitting on the potty-chair. You might let your child manipulate the puppet and talk with you while you're changing diapers. For fun, create a special voice when you use the puppet, and use different voices for different puppets. Don't worry about feeling silly—children don't see the puppet as an extension of you, but as a totally different being. Oven or bath mitts shaped like animals can serve as ready-made puppets, or you can make one of the following simple puppets.

Sock Puppet

Materials:
One old sock (this is a
   great way to use those
   unmatched socks)
Fabric glue
Assorted items to glue onto
   the sock, such as buttons, yarn,
   Easter grass, and sequins

Directions:
1. Place your hand in the sock to help place facial features correctly.
2. Glue items on the sock to make features such as eyes, nose, mouth, and hair.
3. To operate the puppet, stick your hand inside.

Paper Plate Puppet

Materials:
White paper plates
Markers (preferably
   ones that won't
   show through
   the plate)
Optional: Assorted household items
   to glue on, such as buttons and yarn

Directions:
1. Fold paper plate in half. The inside of the crease becomes the mouth of the puppet.
2. Draw features such as eyes, nose, and hair on the top of the plate, or glue on household items to make the face.

Quiet As a Mouse

Do you ever suspect that something has happened at child care that turned your child into a grouch? Children love to talk to puppets and might want to tell this cute little mouse things that they won't tell you directly. Try tucking this puppet into your sleeve or coat pocket. Then, on the ride home, slip out the puppet to whisper in your child's ear. This is an especially useful strategy to use if your child is sad or feeling upset about something. Quietly whispering with the mouse will have a calming affect on your child.

Materials:

Felt—pink and gray or brown
Moveable eyes
Small pom-poms
Glue

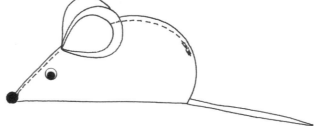

Directions:

1. From the gray or brown felt, cut a heart shape (approximately 4 inches high for the mouse's body, a smaller heart shape for the ears, and a thin strip for the tail.
2. From the pink felt, cut a smaller heart shape for the inside of the ears.
3. Glue the pink heart onto the smaller gray heart to make the ear.
4. Fold the larger heart in half. The sharp point at the base of the heart will be the nose. Fold the ears in half, with the pink side in, and place the ears between the two halves of the body so that the seam will catch them. Sew from the nose end to the back, catching the point of the ear in the seam and leaving the back of the large heart open for your finger. (You can use glue instead of sewing if you prefer.)
5. Attach the tail to the back.
6. Glue the moveable eye and pom-pom nose to the pointed end of the mouse puppet.

Wagon Box

Toddlers love to push and pull things. This simply made wagon is perfect for toddlers to slide along the floor to help clean up toys. Your child will have great fun picking up the toys, putting them in the box, and then pushing or pulling the box over to the shelves to unload them.

Materials:
1 medium-size cardboard box (about 15 by 12 by 10 inches)
Heavy cording, 30 inches long
Colorful self-adhesive paper (enough to cover the box inside and outside)
4 plastic margarine tub covers
4 large brass fasteners
Duct tape

Directions:

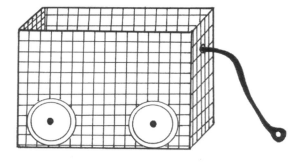

1. Fold the top flaps inside the box to reinforce it. If using a box with a lid, set the box inside the lid for reinforcement.
2. Cover the inside and outside of the box, including the bottom, with decorative paper.
3. Attach the margarine tub covers at each corner with a brass fastener to look like wheels. (For safety, cover the brad on the inside with duct tape.) Make sure the "wheels" are even with the box's bottom edge, so they don't snap off.
4. Make a hole in the middle of one box end and attach the cord. Knot both ends of the cord, one inside the box and one at the pulling end of the cord.

Wiggle Worms

It may sometimes be hard to get children to bed. Make this time more fun by having them get to the bed in an unusual way. For example, ask them if they can crawl to bed like worms, fly like birds, or waddle like ducks. Your children will be snuggled in bed before they know it, and you will be able to leave them on a positive note.

After you've tried this a few times, let your child choose how he or she wants to get to bed. Say something like, "It's bedtime! Would you like to slither like a snake or gallop like a horse tonight?" It's always a good idea to let children choose *how* they are going to do something that's not optional, since you can't let them choose *whether* or not to do it.

Busy Times

Activities for children to do on their own while parents are busy with household responsibilities, such as preparing meals, talking on the telephone, cleaning the house, or studying.

Have you ever heard parents tell stories about what their toddlers "get into" while the adults are talking on the telephone? Young children seem to know when their parents are busy and will get into anything they have ever been told not to touch or do. Yet parents have many tasks that can't involve children. Often, a parent's solution to these times is to turn on the television or stick a video into the VCR.

There is a better solution. The activities in this chapter are things that children can do on their own while parents are busy with their work. Children occupied with their own "work" will be happy to sit in the same room where their mom or dad is working. These activities are also great learning opportunities and fun to do. It is important to explain to parents that these activities are designed to be played with during "special" work times. You might suggest keeping them separate from children's regular toys—this will help the activities to remain novel and capture the children's attention longer.

Activity Boxes

Activity boxes are fun for children to play with while parents are busy cleaning, cooking, studying, or visiting with houseguests. The boxes are quick to put together and best of all, they make use of all the little toys and "collections" children accumulate through the years.

To put a box together, simply gather a collection of similar items such as small stuffed puppies or kitties, plastic dinosaurs, truck-shaped erasers, or colorful plastic fish. Place one collection in a small box such as a lunch box or a school box. If desired, decorate the outside of the box with stickers to match the theme of the items in the box.

Your child can do things such as sort by size or color, or count the items. If you add a die, your older preschooler could roll the die and count out that number of items.

Bat the Ball

Older preschoolers and school-age children will love the challenge of this home-made bat made from a hanger and a knee-high nylon stocking. Paired with a soft foam ball, the bat will keep your child occupied while you attend to your household responsibilities. Encourage your child to play with the bat and ball in an open area where it's okay to move around a lot. See how many times he or she can bounce the ball in the air with the bat without it falling to the ground. Another idea is to take the ball and two bats outside, where two or more children can bounce the ball back and forth.

Materials:
Wire hanger (child size works best although any size will do)
Knee-high nylon stocking
Duct tape

Directions:
1. Pull the bottom of the hanger out until the hanger forms a diamond shape.
2. Bend the hook of the hanger so that you don't have a sharp point.
3. Pull the nylon over the hanger so that the elastic band of the nylon covers the hook.
4. Wrap the duct tape around the nylon-covered hook several times to form the handle of the bat.

Bountiful Beanbags

Keep some of these versatile beanbags on hand for your child to play with while he or she waits for family members to return home at the end of the day. The greatest advantage of these beanbags is that they can be made with items from your home. If you use Styrofoam pellets or aquarium rocks for filling and use thread or waterproof glue to seal them tightly, the glove or mitten beanbags can be washed and dried. Beanbags are also a fun prop to get your child to exercise. Turn off the TV, put on some music, and start moving!

Materials:

Baby sock, stretchy glove (one-
  size-fits-all), or mitten
Filling material, such as popcorn seeds, rice, Styrofoam
  pellets, or aquarium rocks
Yarn
Waterproof glue, hot glue gun,
  or sewing materials

Directions for Sock Beanbag:

1. Pour the filler of your choice into half of the sock foot.
2. Tie the sock into a single knot at the heel and turn the cuff of the sock down, so that it surrounds the part with the filler (this gives the beanbag double durability).
3. Gather the top of the cuff together. Using a small strand of yarn, tie a double knot around the gathered section.

Directions for Glove or Mitten Beanbag:

1. Pour filler into the stretchy glove or mitten until it is approximately ¾ full.
2. Glue the opening at the wrist with waterproof glue or a hot glue gun, or sew the opening securely.

Bowl of Dough

Play dough is always a favorite with children. It can keep a child occupied for long periods of time while you are busy cooking dinner, studying, doing laundry, or writing out bills. Your child will be even more thrilled with his or her very own Bowl of Dough that doesn't have to be shared with anyone. Just gather a variety of utensils such as a plastic pizza cutter, plastic knives, a Popsicle stick, and a rolling pin, and store them in a box or a bag with a small amount of dough. For easy cleanup, give your child a foam-rubber place mat to play on. You can purchase play dough or make your own with the recipe provided below.

Materials:
1 cup flour
½ cup salt
1 Tablespoon vegetable oil
2 teaspoons cream of tartar
1 cup water
food coloring

Directions:
1. In a medium-size cooking pot, stir together the flour, salt, and cream of tartar.
2. Put food coloring in water. More food coloring will produce darker-color play dough and less food coloring will produce lighter-color play dough. For brilliant or very dark colors, use cake-decorating color.
3. Stir the water into the flour mixture, blending well. Place over medium heat and stir constantly until the dough thickens and pulls away from the side of the pot. The dough is done when it appears dry and no longer sticks to the spoon.
4. Immediately take it out of the pot. When it is cool enough to touch, knead until smooth. Store in covered container or a plastic bag.

Box-o-Rocks

What child doesn't love rocks? A very simple busy-time activity consists of a box of rocks.

Simply find or purchase smooth rocks of varying sizes and colors. You can also purchase a bag of inexpensive, colorful plastic rocks at a craft store. Place the rocks in a decorated lunch box or school box.

Your child will love taking the rocks out of the box to count or to sort by color or size.

Warning: This activity is not appropriate for toddlers who like to place small items in their mouths.

Bucket of Magnetic Shapes

Your child will love this toy, and you will be delighted to find how inexpensive and easy it is to make. The bucket is just an old peanut butter container decorated with stickers. It is filled with the metal caps (also decorated with stickers) that come on bottles of juice or the metal lids from cans of frozen juice concentrate. The latter are good for toddlers because they are too big to choke on. For a handy way to store the wand, attach a piece of hooked fabric such as Velcro to the magnetic wand, and a looped piece to the side of the bucket.

Your child will become captivated dipping the wand into the bucket to see how many caps cling to the wand. The noise and feel of the caps will especially appeal to toddlers. If colored stickers are placed on the lids, they can be sorted or matched. Two children can play together by taking turns pulling lids out of the bucket to find a match.

Materials:
Empty plastic peanut butter
   bucket (or any com-
   parable bucket)
Metal caps from glass jars, or
   lids from frozen juice cans
Magnetic wand (available in
   school-supply stores and
   fabric stores)
Optional: Stickers
         Velcro dots

Directions:
1. Decorate the outside of the bucket with a variety of stickers, if desired.
2. Place stickers of different shapes and colors on the metal caps (one per cap), if desired.
3. Place the caps and the wand inside the bucket.

Parent Pointer
BUSY TIMES

Circle of Match-Ups

Make this game for your child to build fine-motor skills and matching abilities. Choose stickers related to a topic that interests your child, such as trucks or dinosaurs. Your child's job is to find the matching stickers around the edge of the circle and clip a matching pair of clothespins on top of the stickers.

Materials:
Cardboard circle, 10 to 12 inches across; the cardboard circle from a frozen pizza works well
Stickers in matching pairs (10 to 20 pairs per circle)
Clothespins (2 for each pair of stickers)
Resealable plastic bag, to store the clothespins
Fine-point permanent markers
Optional: Brass fastener

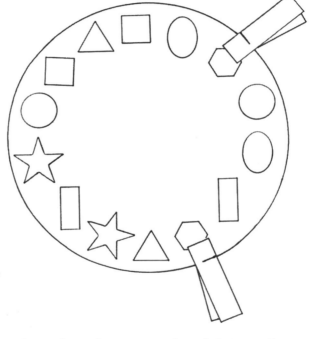

Directions:
1. Select pairs of matching stickers and place them around the outer edge of the cardboard circle. Try to space them evenly, and mix up the matching pairs.
2. Using the fine-point permanent markers, draw shapes or colored dots on the clothespins. Make two clothespins of each color, so that you have the same number of pairs of clothespins as you do pairs of stickers.
3. Place the clothespins in resealable plastic bag and, if desired, attach the bag to the cardboard circle by punching the brass fastener through the corner of the plastic bag and through the cardboard circle.

Parent Pointer
BUSY TIMES

Fill-and-Dump Fun

One of a toddler's favorite activities is filling a container up and dumping it out again. Bring out a container (box, basket, bowl, bucket, etc.) and five or six items for your child to put in it while you are occupied with studying, household chores, or cooking. Keep the items simple. Make sure the items are durable so they cannot be bitten off, and large enough so they will not be swallowed. Examples of items to place in the container might be plastic blocks, sponges, net body-scrubbers, plastic animals, small stuffed animals, and large pom-poms.

You don't have to spend a lot of money on this fun activity. Remember that sometimes toddlers enjoy the box more than the expensive toy that came in it.

Limiting the contents of the container to five or six items will speed cleanup once you are done with your chores and ready to spend time with your child. Make the fill-and-dump items available only during these special times, so that your toddler doesn't tire of them.

Glove Clackers and Ringers

What fun your child will have doing this stretching activity while you are busy cooking dinner or cleaning the house! Make this toy by securely sewing buttons and large jingle bells on a child-size glove. Look in Grandma's button box or craft and fabric stores for large colorful buttons. Show your child how to tap the buttons together to make a clacking sound and shake his or her hand to ring the bells. After you've made the glove and practiced making sounds, put some music on and let your child shake, jingle, and clack while you clean the house. This is a good activity for hand coordination, leg muscles, and exercising the whole body as the child moves to the music.

Materials:
Child-size glove (one-size-fits-all stretch gloves work well)
Buttons
Jingle bells
Heavy-duty thread (thread for making jewelry, purchased at craft
  stores, works perfectly)
Needle

Directions:
1. Sew a button on the inside tip of each finger and the inside of the thumb.
2. Sew three or four bells around the wristband of the glove. Tug on these after they are sewn, to make sure they cannot be pulled off.

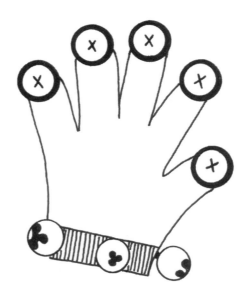

Junk Box

A junk box put together just for your child (a safe version of the adult junk drawer found in nearly every home) is sure to pique curiosity and occupy your child while you are talking on the phone, busy with a houseguest, or doing household chores. If you are sitting close to each other, your child can ask you questions about the items or show you what he or she can do with them.

Some items to include in the junk box are a magnifying glass, a miniature kaleidoscope, a small book, and a squishy stress ball. The possibilities are almost endless. Nature stores have very interesting items that you can throw into a junk box. This is also a great place to put those little toys that your child receives in children's meals from fast-food restaurants. For the box, use a small lunch box or a school pencil box with a lid.

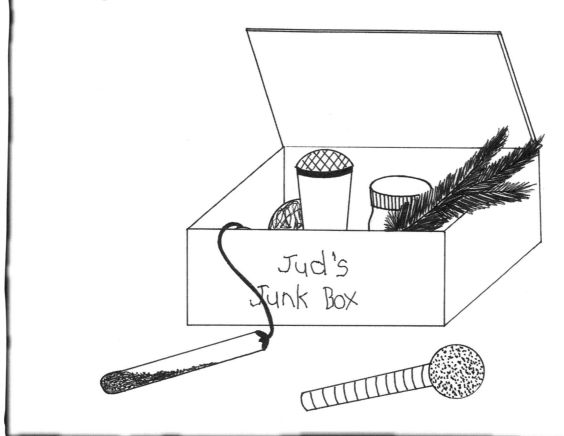

Lids in a Tube

Young children love to empty containers and fill them up over and over again. This simple activity, consisting of a tennis ball container and juice-can lids, will keep your child occupied while you are busy with laundry, cooking, or cleaning around the house. And the best thing about this activity is that it is made entirely from reused materials. Collect the tin lids from frozen juice containers and stack them in an empty tennis ball container. The lids are a perfect fit, so the container becomes a simple shape sorter. Your child can pour out the lids, count them, stack them, or drop them back into the container one by one. To add a challenge, place stickers on the lids (either pictures or plain colored dots will work) for your child to sort and match. Your child will not tire of this toy as easily if you get it out periodically instead of including it in the regular toy collection.

Materials:
Empty tennis ball container
Lids from 12-ounce frozen juice containers
Stickers or colored sticky dots

Directions:
1. Place stickers on lids to make matching sets. Older preschoolers might enjoy matching lids that have dots placed in patterns like the dots on dice.
2. Stack lids in the empty tennis ball container.

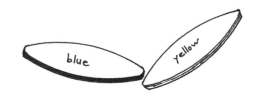

Nesting Bowls

One of a toddler's favorite activities is to play with real dishes, just like moms and dads. A set of nesting bowls that fit inside each other will provide lots of opportunities to do just that. If you use a plastic set with lids, your child can strengthen fine-motor skills by removing the lid from each bowl and pulling out the next. When they are all taken apart, your child can put them back together again, which is a little more challenging.

For toddlers, you will want to put just the bowls out, without the lids, since it might be a little too challenging for them to put the lids back on. Or put the lids on the bowls and stack them into a tower. Toddlers will love to knock them over and start again.

Place a wooden spoon with the nesting bowls to use for beating on the bowls as if they were drums. The different sounds of the various sizes of bowls will be an interesting sensory experience for them. Or fill one bowl with manipulatives such as plastic blocks, small stuffed animals, or plastic links. Give it to your toddler while waiting for a sibling to arrive home from school or while waiting for dinner to be prepared, to help keep the toddler busy during those difficult waiting times.

Peek-a-Boo Box

Did you ever notice that a child sometimes enjoys the box a gift comes in more than the toy inside? Your child will love the cozy little space you create in this crawl-through box with peek-a-boo openings. Your toddler will love to look through the holes and play peek-a-boo with you. Your preschooler will enjoy looking at a book or playing with small stuffed animals in her "hide-away" while you prepare supper. On a really special day, your child can take a blanket in for a nap. Keep the box "magical" by putting it out only at certain times. When it's not in use, flatten it for the next rainy day when your child needs to release some pent-up energy indoors.

Materials:
Large cardboard box (big enough for your child to crawl through)
Nontoxic spray paint, colored self-adhesive paper, or permanent markers
Utility knife

Directions:

1. Fold the end flaps all the way inside the box. Note: DO NOT cut the flaps off the box—it will collapse.
2. If desired, take the box outside and spray it with nontoxic spray paint, cover the outside with self-adhesive paper, or let your child decorate it with permanent markers (under your supervision).
3. Use the utility knife to cut small shapes out of the side of the box at various intervals. The shapes should be large enough for the child to peek through.

Pizza-Box Felt Board

Children love to hear and tell stories, and storytelling is a wonderful way to promote language skills. This felt board will encourage your child to create stories at home. The storytelling pieces will stick to the felt to illustrate the story, and they are kept neat and organized inside the box when not in use. Your child can sit at the table while you are cooking dinner, studying, or paying bills, and make up stories to tell you. After dinner you can switch roles and make up stories to tell your child. Your child will especially love hearing stories about when you were young. They will be stories your child will remember for life!

Materials:

Pizza box

Large piece of felt to fit inside
  of pizza box lid

Glue

Felt or heavyweight sew-in
  interfacing material for story
  telling pieces

Fabric markers

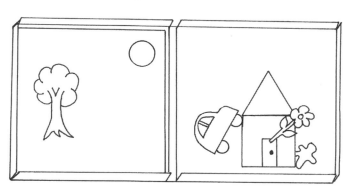

Directions:

1. To make the storytelling pieces, draw basic shapes onto felt or interfacing material; use scrap paper to make patterns first if you prefer. You might include trees, sun, flowers, boy, girl, cat, dog, house, fruits, vegetables, car, truck, and plane.
2. Cut the shapes out and use the fabric markers to add details such as features on faces or windows and doors on buildings. The heavyweight interfacing material is particularly easy to draw details onto.
3. To make the felt board, cut one large piece of felt to fit the inside of the pizza box lid, and glue it in place.

©2001 *Transition Magician for Families;* Redleaf Press, 450 North Syndicate, Suite 5, St. Paul, MN 55104, 800-423-8309

Playing on the Wall

While you're on the phone, making supper, or writing out bills, keep your child busy with this fun activity. Gather a variety of children's magnets such as letters, numbers, and assorted shapes. You could even use fun refrigerator magnets, as long as they don't have small pieces that will break off. Let your child spell out names, order and sort the magnets, or even create stories out of the magnets. The magnets can be played with on the side of the refrigerator, metal filing cabinet, metal shelf, or even a metal door.

Store the magnets out of sight, and get them out just for these special times so that your child will not tire of them.

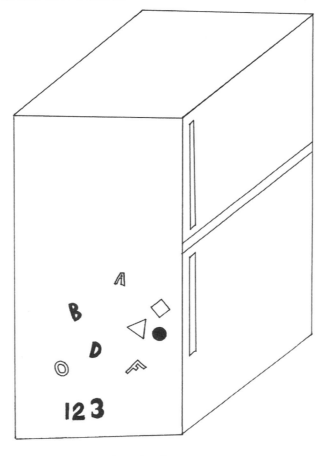

©2001 *Transition Magician for Families*; Redleaf Press, 450 North Syndicate, Suite 5, St. Paul, MN 55104, 800-423-8309

Puzzle Put-Togethers

Simple puzzles made from household materials are a great activity for your child to do independently while you do paperwork or study. Because they are made from inexpensive materials, it will not be a costly loss if one piece disappears, as so often happens with puzzles. You can adapt the puzzles to match your child's developmental level. A two- to three-piece puzzle is appropriate for a young toddler to begin with, while an eight- to ten-piece puzzle is a good starting place for a young preschooler. As your child masters a puzzle, simply cut it into more pieces to make it more challenging. The directions below explain how to make puzzles from empty cereal or other food boxes, sponge-backed pot scrubbers, or foam-rubber place mats. Place each puzzle in its own resealable plastic bag for easy storage.

Materials:
Empty cereal or other cardboard
  boxes, rectangular sponge-backed
  pot scrubbers (available in assorted
  colors), or foam-rubber place mat
Clear Con-Tact paper (if using boxes)
Resealable plastic bags

Directions:
1. Cut the cardboard, place mat, or pot scrubber into the desired number of pieces.
2. If using cardboard, cover both sides of each puzzle piece with clear Con-Tact paper for added strength.
3. Store individual puzzles in plastic bags.

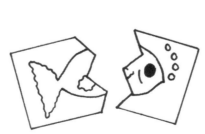

Sound Jars

These sound jars make good use of all those 35 mm film canisters you have in the back of your junk drawer. Your child will enjoy shaking them to find the pairs with the matching sounds. When your child tires of one set of sound jars, make a new set with different filler materials to challenge your child all over again. For every matching pair of sound jars, draw matching colored dots or use matching colored sticky dots on the bottom of the jar. Your child can check the dots for a correct match. Store the sound jars in a small shoe box or resealable plastic bag.

Materials:
35 mm film canisters
Quick-bond glue
Assorted filler material such as rice, sand, salt, popcorn, dried beans, pennies, or small erasers
Permanent markers in assorted colors

Directions:
1. Fill two canisters with identical filler materials. Fill canisters no more than ¼ full so there is room for the material to move around inside and make noise.
2. Glue the lid onto the canister with quick-bond glue.
3. With permanent markers, draw large colored dots on the bottoms of the canisters to indicate matching sets.

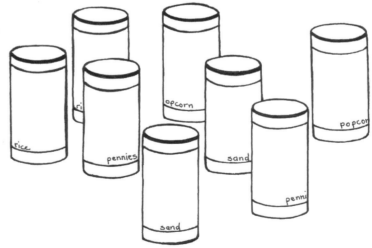

©2001 *Transition Magician for Families*; Redleaf Press, 450 North Syndicate, Suite 5, St. Paul, MN 55104, 800-423-8309

Sponge Pom-pom Balls

Your child will love these colorful pom-pom balls made from sponges, and they help develop eye-hand coordination. The balls are easy and inexpensive, so you can make several. Their light weight allows your child to play ball indoors. Attach a large rubber band to the ball to turn it into a mini punching ball. These are great entertainment for your child while you prepare supper or do the laundry.

Note: A toddler may be able to bite off pieces of the sponge and should be supervised carefully while playing with this toy.

Materials:

3 soft foam sponges per ball (multiple colors create a nice effect)

1 or 2 large, heavy-duty rubber bands (14 inches around) per ball (one rubber band is optional for a handle)

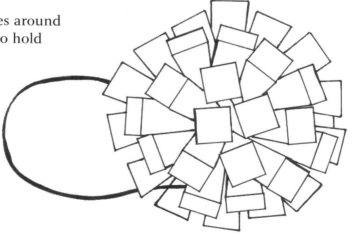

Sponge—cut into four lengths

Directions:

1. Cut each sponge lengthwise into 4 equal strips (see illustration)
2. Gather 12 strips into a bunch.
3. Wrap a rubber band several times around the center of the sponge strips to hold them securely together.
4. Optional: Wrap the second rubber band once around the first rubber band, looping one end through the other, and pull securely down to form a handle (see illustration).

Swing and Sway with Scarves

There is something magical and soothing about dancing with scarves. It is especially interesting if the scarves come in a variety of materials such as silk or sheer fabric. They seem to float through the air.

Encourage your child to twirl them through the air overhead or in front of his or her body; this will help your child develop muscles and recognize positions in space. A scarf for each hand creates some interesting movement.

Put on some quiet music and let the child dance in front of a mirror while you attend to your household chores. Search through dresser drawers for those forgotten scarves, or ask Grandma if she has some that she's not using anymore.

Together Times

Quality activities for parent and child to do together when they are in between the routines of the day.

Early childhood professionals may find it fairly easy to think of creative activities to do with young children. They have been trained in what is developmentally appropriate to do with toddlers and preschoolers, and have a store of ideas built up from years of working with children. But this is not always an easy task for parents of preschoolers who are not trained in the early childhood profession. Long periods of time with young children can sometimes be quite daunting, and parents often rely on child care teachers for ideas about what to do during those times.

The activities in this chapter are designed for parents and children to do together. By offering them, you can support parents in learning how to interact with their children in a nurturing and productive fashion. These are great activities for weekends, rainy or snowy days at home, summer vacations, or even quiet evenings at home. You might want to have a display of sample activities ready to show parents prior to these times of the year.

All Right, Puffs of White

Take time to watch the clouds, smell the roses, and relax with your child. On a warm sunny day, take a blanket outside, lie on your backs, and watch the clouds move. If possible, lay the blanket near a bed of flowers to stimulate the sense of smell also.

Encourage your child to use his or her imagination to describe the forms that are seen in the clouds and the scents in the air. Some clouds look like animals, people, familiar objects, and unusual creatures.

As you relax, this is a perfect time to talk with your child. Tell your child how you feel about him or her, how special he or she is to you.

Animal Hunt

Is your child attracted to those stuffed animals that make noises when you push the hidden button? Use these stuffed animals to play a listening version of hide-and-seek with your child at home. Your home will be filled with laughter by the time the game is over.

Have your child hide with the stuffed animal somewhere in the house. Sing the following phrase to the tune of "Where is Thumbkin?": "Where is (your child's name or the name of the animal), where is (your child's name or the name of the animal)?" The child answers by singing, "Here I am, here I am." While answering, the child pushes the button on the animal to make its noise. Search slowly for your child, and remind the child to keep pressing the button while you search. Have fun!

If you don't have the time to play this hide-and-seek game with your child, hide the animal someplace in your house and let your child search for it while you are engaging in your daily responsibilities. When your child finds it, cheer joyfully, and hide it again.

Beneath the Bowl

Make use of all those extra margarine bowls that accumulate quickly. Turn three or four of the bowls upside down. Choose a skill your child is learning, such as colors, shapes, or numbers. Color, draw, or write the symbols on the bottoms of the bowls with permanent markers. Now take a penny or any small object and place it under one of the bowls while your child has his or her eyes shut. Have your child open his or her eyes and guess which bowl the object is under by naming the color, shape, or numeral. Lift that bowl up to see if the guess was right! If not, guess again until the object is found.

Your child will enjoy doing this over and over. This is a fun activity to do with your child at the kitchen table while you are waiting for dinner to finish cooking. If you use pennies, let your child keep them to put in a piggy bank.

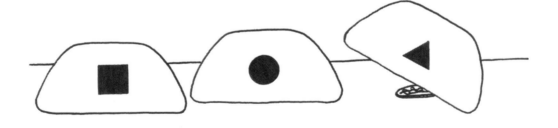

Bottle of Names

Many children's relatives and friends live across the United States or in another country. Help your child feel connected to people, whether they live down the street or far away, with this "Bottle of Names." Write the names of grandparents, aunts and uncles, cousins, and special friends on strips of cardboard with a ribbon attached. When you have a quiet moment at home, have your child pull a name out of the bottle and find a way to connect with that person. Give them a call on the phone, have your child draw a picture to send, or let the child dictate a message to send via e-mail. This activity can be special for all involved.

Materials:
Plastic bottle with large mouth, such
  as a medium-size peanut butter jar
File folder, index cards, or poster
  board
Narrow satin ribbon
Marker
Scissors
Paper punch

Directions:
1. Cut 1-by-5-inch strips of file folders, index cards, or poster board.
2. Print the name of a relative or a friend on each of the strips.
3. Punch a hole in one end of each strip.
4. Cut ribbon into approximately 9-inch lengths (or simply long enough to hang over the top of the jar) and tie through the hole in each strip.
5. Put the strips in the bottle and let the colorful ribbons hang over the edge.

Box Balancing

Get your child moving with these fun box activities.

Your toddler will want to do this balancing game over and over. Start with one little box and ask the child to put it on top of his or her head and balance it there until you count to three. Say, "One, two, three, drop!" Then when you say, "Drop," the child will let it fall to the ground, then eagerly pick it up and do it all over again.

Ask the child to balance it on other parts of his or her body—foot, elbow, or hand. This is a good activity to see if your child recognizes varying body parts. There is also a lot of eye-hand coordination skill building as your child bends to pick up the box and balances it.

As your child gets older, collect more small boxes. Have the child try to balance a box or two on his or her head while walking around. The child will also enjoy stacking them and knocking them over.

Develop your child's brain by taking the boxes apart and having the child match the tops with the bottoms. The child will probably find a treasure or two to put in the boxes too. It's amazing what you and your child will find to do with a bunch of little boxes.

Box of Mementos

Children are always collecting small items such as rocks, whistles, stuffed animals, balls, photos of special people in their lives, and so on. Often, these treasures get stuffed into pockets, collect in junk drawers, or slip under the bed only to get sucked up by the vacuum. Even worse, they are forgotten, and many wonderful memories are lost forever.

Find and label a special box (such as a pencil box or a cigar box) to store these collectibles. Then, when your child is sick in bed, or bored because of blustery weather outside, get out the box of mementos and explore them together. Take the box with you when you eat out at a restaurant. Let your child explore the items while you wait for your food to arrive. This activity is sure to spark conversations about the past.

Cards with Peek Holes

This is a perfect way to reuse an old greeting card. Fold the card so that the picture is on the inside. Punch or cut holes in strategic places on the top flap. Strategic places might be over a teddy bear's eye, or a flower's petals. Have children guess what the picture is, then open it to see if the guess was correct.

Collect some cards, punch the holes, and store them in a small bag. Pull the bag out when you have a quiet moment at home, such as when you are waiting for a ride or for the rest of the family to arrive home at the end of the day. See if your child can figure out the pictures by peeking through the holes.

Once your child easily recognizes the first set of cards, make new ones, and start the guessing again. Take time to read the greetings and the signatures on the cards, and recall those special people and events in your child's life.

Parent Pointer
TOGETHER TIMES

Cuddle Up a Little

One way to end a busy day is to cuddle up a little with your child. Decorate a blanket or a towel together by drawing on it with permanent markers or fabric paint. Let your child draw any design desired. Be sure to sign each of your names on the blanket.

Use the blanket or towel while singing songs, while reading a book, to help calm a sick child, or before bedtime while talking about the day. Make a special blanket or towel for each of your children, or choose a blanket that's big enough for three or four of you to cuddle up in. This time spent with your child can be relaxing for both of you.

Dots

Dots is an old game that can keep children occupied for long periods of time. To play, children take turns drawing lines to connect two dots. When a square is made, the child connecting the last line puts his or her initials inside the square. The game continues until all the dots are connected. To start a new game, simply wipe the board clean with a tissue and start again. Enjoy playing this game with your child on those rainy days or while supper is baking.

Materials:
Poster board or file folder
Mini shape stickers (such as
   sticky dots, hearts, smiley faces
   or washable markers)
Clear Con-Tact paper
Overhead transparency marker
Tissues
Small plastic bags
Brass paper fastener

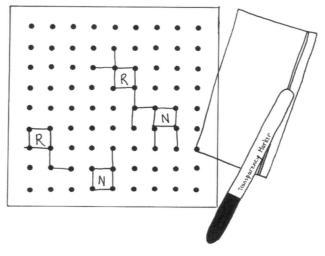

Directions:
1. Cut the poster board or file folder into a square (approximately 10 by 10 inches).
2. Place stickers in five rows of five each so that the stickers are evenly spaced with each other (see illustration), or draw small dots with the nonpermanent marker in the same pattern.
3. Cover with clear Con-Tact paper.
4. Place an overhead-transparency marker and tissues in a small plastic bag. Attach to a corner of the game board with the paper fastener.

Family Photo Fun

Children never seem to tire of playing games like "Family Photo Fun." Pictures of family members are especially appealing to them. Substitute magazine cutouts or small calendar pictures if photos are not available.

Lay four or five pictures on the table. Have your child shut his or her eyes. Take a picture away. Open up! Have your child guess which picture is missing.

For added fun, reverse roles, letting your child take the picture away.

This is a good activity to do as you spend some quality time with your child. Take some time to talk about the special people in the photos.

Favorite Things to Do

Create an "Our Favorite Things to Do" bag at home with your child.

Decide together on some of your favorite things to do together. Cut out or draw pictures for each favorite thing, such as telling a story, playing the "I Spy" game, or saying rhymes with hand actions like "The Itsy-Bitsy Spider." Mount the pictures on cards and put them in a special bag. If activities require props, include them in the bag too. If you want to encourage reading, add words to the cards.

When when you have a few extra minutes, before dinner, before bedtime, or before swim lessons, pull out your bag and let your child choose a card, then do the activity together. It makes the time fly by.

Flashy Flashlights

There is something about flashlights that children are drawn to. Put a little magic and fun into reading books before bed by turning off the lights and reading by flashlight. Your child will love it! You can pretend you are on a camping trip. Mini lights that attach to books are fun, too.

Soft lighting is relaxing and can be soothing before bedtime. Make a special flashlight just for you and your child to use by decorating the flashlight with stickers.

Message in an Egg

Don't put those plastic eggs away after Easter. Write short love notes or special activity ideas to your child on a strip of paper and place one in each egg. Present your child with an egg when you wake her in the morning, leave it by her place setting at the dinner table, or hide it in her room and let her search for it. Another idea is to place several eggs in a basket and let her choose one each day. "Message in an Egg" promotes self-esteem and creates wonderful family memories.

Here are some examples of messages you might use:

I have a bear hug for you today.
Ask me why you make me happy.
Choose your favorite book and we'll read it today.
Let's plan a trip to the park.
I love you!
Let's build something with your blocks.

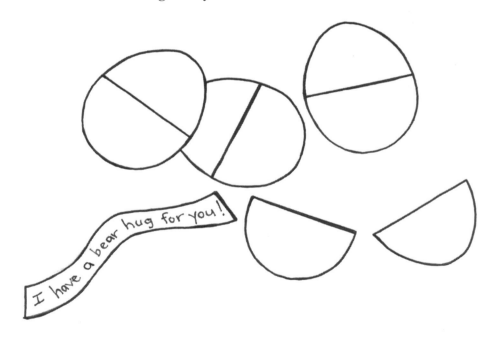

I have a bear hug for you!

Parent Pointer
TOGETHER TIMES

Packing Up

Ask your child to help you fill a lunch box or picnic basket with items you would pack for a lunch, such as plate, cup, plastic spoon and fork, napkin, tablecloth, drink bag, raisin box, and other snacks. Use items you might have for lunch at your house.

Ask your child to name each item as you put them into the box. Close the lid of the lunch box and ask your child to tell you what is in the box. When he or she correctly identifies an item, take it out of the lunch box. When the guessing is done, have an impromptu picnic with your child!

You could use the same idea with a small suitcase and a trip to grandma's house. This is a perfect game to help your child's brain develop, because of the language and memory skills involved.

Pinhole Wand

Turn off the television and take a walk. To make this walk more special than usual, take some pinhole wands with you. These wands are simple to make, so go ahead and make one for each family member.

Explore the neighborhood through a tiny hole. This allows you and your child to focus on a small portion of a tree, a flower, or the sky. You'll be surprised what you can see through the pinhole. Added benefits include time to talk with your child, exercise, and stimulate brain development. If the weather doesn't allow you to be outside, take a walk around the house.

Materials:
Poster board
Scissors
Paper punch or pin
Popsicle stick
Glue
Optional: Con-Tact paper

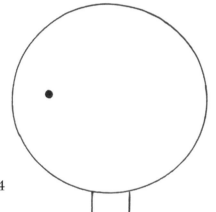

Directions:
1. Cut a circle from poster board, approximately 4 inches in diameter.
2. Cover both sides with self-adhesive paper, such as Con-Tact paper (this is optional).
3. Glue the end of a Popsicle stick onto the circle to form a handle.
4. Poke a hole about half an inch from one edge of the circle with a paper punch, or by poking it with a pin.

Shaker Bottles

Reuse those empty soft-drink bottles! Make a set of shaker bottles with your child. Each bottle will sound different when you fill them with various items from around the house. Choose the right bottle size for your child's age and developmental level. For instance, small juice bottles are perfect for toddlers, and 20-ounce soft-drink or water bottles are a good size for preschoolers. You can also use baby bottles that are no longer needed for drinking. While you are on the treadmill or exercise bike, put on some music, get out the shaker bottles, and let your child shake and exercise right beside you.

Materials:
Empty plastic bottles (water, soft-drink, juice, or baby bottles)
Filler items such as noodles, rice, popcorn, paper clips, spare nuts and bolts, pennies, etc. (check the junk drawer for some unique fillers)
Fingernail polish remover (acetone)
Superglue
Tape player and musical tapes
Optional: Stickers

Directions:
1. Remove labels from bottles and clean off excess glue with fingernail polish remover.
2. Pour or drop approximately ½ inch of filler into the bottle.
3. Drip two or three drops of superglue onto the ridges inside the cap and screw on the bottle.
4. Optional: Decorate the outside of the bottle with stickers.

©2001 *Transition Magician for Families*; Redleaf Press, 450 North Syndicate, Suite 5, St. Paul, MN 55104, 800-423-8309

Super Streamers

There are few things children love more than singing and dancing. Your child will enjoy these inexpensive and easy-to-make props. Streamers can be made with various materials around the house. Tape streamers on a Popsicle stick or tie them on a hoop. They are colorful and make delightful sounds. On a rainy afternoon, push back the rug, put on some music, and let your child dance away. Better yet, grab a streamer and dance along with your child.

Materials:
Popsicle sticks or unsharpened pencil (for stick version)
Shower curtain rings or margarine tub lids (for ring version)
Streamer material such as garbage or bread bags, curling ribbon, tinsel, etc., in
  lengths of 12 to 24 inches
Electrician's tape
Scissors

Directions: Streamers on a Stick

1. Cut garbage or bread bags into 1-inch-wide strips if you're choosing that material for your streamer.
2. Cut a piece of electrician's tape approximately 6 inches long and lay it on the table, sticky side up.
3. Adhere the ends of 4 or 5 streamers to the strip of electrician's tape, leaving 1 inch open on each end of the tape.
4. Wrap the tape around the end of the Popsicle stick or unsharpened pencil.

Directions: Streamers on a Hoop

1. Cut garbage or bread bags into 1-inch-wide strips if you're choosing that material for your streamer.
2. Cut the inside out of a margarine tub lid, leaving approximately ½ inch for an edge if you're choosing that material for your hoop. Wrap the hoop with electrician's tape. Skip this step if you're using the shower curtain ring for a hoop.
3. Gather 4 or 5 streamers together and knot them onto the hoop.

On the Move

Activities for children to do while traveling, both on the everyday trip to school or child care, and on longer trips.

In today's transient society, parents and children spend a substantial amount of time traveling by car, bus, train, and even plane. The activities in this chapter will be very useful for families in your program who have a long commute to work and school, or who spend a lot of time traveling on weekends or holidays. These activities will help the time fly by when children and parents are traveling together. Some of the activities are for children to do alone if the parent is busy driving, while others work as great conversation starters and will promote children's language development.

Parent Pointer
ON THE MOVE

ABC's in a Bag

For your older preschooler, take a bag of alphabet cards with you when you're on the move. Use the time while waiting at bus or plane terminals, or while driving in the car, to work on letter recognition.

Have your child draw a card from the alphabet bag. Ask the child to identify the letter, then to think of words that begin with that letter.

You might also ask him or her to find objects in your immediate surroundings that begin with that same letter.

Color Cards

Traveling can involve lots of hurrying up and lots of waiting. Waiting for trains, planes, and buses is difficult for adults and even more so for children. Make these quick little color cards to pull out of a bag just for these times. Color cards are simply strips cut from file folders in different colors, kept on a ring for handy use. They are made small so that you can slide them in and out of your pocket. Show your child one color at a time and have him or her find something in the area that is that color, or think of something that is that color. Having a card to look at while you say the name of the color is a great help for toddlers who are just learning their colors. Some file folders come with bright colors on one side and a pastel tint of the same color on the other side. Use these to double the use of the color cards.

Materials:
File folders in six different colors
Clear Con-Tact paper
Paper punch (shape punches, such as a star or a heart, are a fun variation)
Metal ring, 1 inch in diameter

Directions:
1. Cut file folders into 1-by-6-inch strips.
2. Cover the file folder pieces with Con-Tact paper.
3. Punch a hole in one end of each strip in the same spot. Hold the strips together by inserting the metal ring through the holes.

Emotions Song

Children need to learn that everyone, including moms and dads, feels all kinds of emotions at different times. Make good use of uninterrupted time while driving together in the car to talk and sing together about feelings. Singing songs showing different emotions would be a good opener to talking about feelings with your child.

Simply pick one of your favorite songs and sing it with you child. Talk to your child about how someone sounds when they are sad, tired, angry, and so on. Now sing with your child as though you are sad, then scared, shy, angry, and so on. Pick any emotion you can pretend to be.

Be sure to talk to your child about the idea that this is "pretend." Young children, particularly toddlers, rely on you to be a stable, calm person for them at all times.

After singing the song, talk about some of the things that make you and your child feel sad, angry, scared, and so on.

Parent Pointer
ON THE MOVE

Fun Fanny Pack

Anticipate those on-the-go, have-to-wait moments with your child by wearing a fun fanny pack filled with interesting items.

Start by selecting an unusual fanny pack that will pique your child's attention. Then fill it with items such as small books you can read to your child, a magnifying glass, stickers with pictures that will initiate familiar songs, a bottle of bubbles to blow, or finger puppets.

Change to a different fanny pack periodically, and change the contents more often. The unexpected waiting time if the bus is late or the commuter train breaks down will go quickly when you are prepared! And a child who gets to take a turn wearing the fun fanny pack now and then will feel pretty special.

Love Tickets

If you have several children who argue in the back seat of the car, try playing this game throughout the trip. For every kind deed, obedient response, or sincerely loving gesture, a child receives a "love ticket." The tickets are simply small slips of plain paper—you'll need 10 to 20 per child. Each ticket earned is placed in a small paper bag with that child's name on it. The bags can be taped to the dashboard, or placed wherever they will be convenient.

After accumulating a certain number of tickets, the child can cash them in for a prize. For example:

    2 tickets = 1 sticker

    4 tickets = 1 special snack

    6 tickets = a small toy

    8 tickets = a box of crayons

    10 tickets = a storybook

Before you start your trip, explain to your children exactly which behaviors will result in being given a ticket, and which ones will not.

Magical Melodies

Give your child's teacher or child care provider a blank audiocassette tape and ask the teacher to tape the children singing their favorite songs at group time. Play the tape while you are driving along in the car for you and your child to sing along to. It will help the time pass quickly. Your child will love it when you learn his or her favorite songs from school.

For a variation, tape sounds in your home, voices of family members (grandparents and relatives from a distance are wonderful), or animal sounds. Have your child guess the sound or voice as you drive along. This would be a nice tape for your child to take along to child care and listen to when feeling lonely.

Magnetic Fingertips

This fascinating toy is a good choice to tuck into a backpack for long trips. The effect of the magnets on metal items floating in oil is mesmerizing for all small children, but it is especially relaxing for those who are under stress. The child puts on a glove with magnets attached and rubs the fingertips along the sides of the bottle. When the child pulls the glove away from the bottle, the items will float slowly to the bottom. For children under three, you may want to use a thin mitten or sock instead of a glove.

Materials:
Clear plastic 20-ounce soft-drink bottle, thoroughly cleaned and dried out
Fingernail polish remover (acetone) and rag
Baby oil, enough to fill the bottle almost full
Metal items such as paper clips, pipe cleaners, tacks, push pins, safety pins, or bingo chips with metal rims
Superglue
Electrician's tape
Children's garden glove or one-size-fits-all stretchy knit glove
5 strong magnets (can be purchased at craft stores)

Directions:
1. From a clear plastic soft-drink bottle, remove all labels and clean off label glue with fingernail polish remover and a rag. Make sure the bottle is cleaned out and dried thoroughly, because any moisture left in the bottle will rust the metal pieces.
2. Drop several metal items in the bottle and fill the bottle full with baby oil.
3. Drip superglue around the inside of the cap and tightly screw it on the bottle. Seal the cap on with electrician's tape.
4. Glue magnets onto the fingertips of the glove with superglue. Be sure to test this toy before counting on it to calm your child, because it may take several tries to find strong enough magnets.

©2001 *Transition Magician for Families;* Redleaf Press, 450 North Syndicate, Suite 5, St. Paul, MN 55104, 800-423-8309

Mini Microphone

Do you ever sing along to the radio while you drive? Turn this into a fun activity for your child by making this simple mini microphone. Children love to imitate the performers they have seen, and your child will love putting on a show for you as you travel. Everyone in the car could take turns singing into the microphone, or you could make several—they are small enough to fit easily into the glove compartment.

Materials:
Sponge ball (a cat toy works well)
Pencil with eraser top
Glue

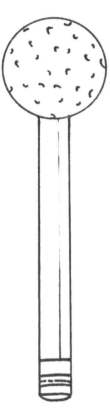

Directions:
1. Make a small slit in the sponge ball, just big enough to fit the pencil into.
2. Put a small amount of glue on the lead end of the pencil and insert it into the hole in the ball.

   Note: The eraser of the pencil provides a soft, safe end for toddlers to hold.

Parent Pointer
ON THE MOVE

Pillow Pleasantries

If you have an early-morning commute to child care, or if you frequently go on longer car trips (such as trips to visit grandparents), take along this special travel pillow for your child. Follow the directions below for making the pillow. An old bed sheet or favorite blanket that is getting ragged around the edges will make a very nice pillow.

Materials:
Two pieces of fabric, for the two
   sides of the pillow
Permanent markers, fabric markers,
   or fabric paint
Polyester fiberfill

Directions:
1. Have your child decorate a piece of fabric using permanent markers, fabric markers, or fabric paint. If using fabric paint, allow to dry.

2. With right sides together, place the decorated piece of fabric on top of a second piece of fabric, which will be the back of the pillow. (You can also place the right sides facing out, cut around the child's design, and then flip the fabric so that right sides are together. Just make sure you cut so that the two sides will match correctly.) Cut into any shape desired, cutting both pieces at the same time. Ask your child to help decide on the shape and size.

3. Sew around the edges using ½-inch seam, leaving a small space for turning.

4. Turn the pillow right side out, and stuff it with polyester fiberfill. Stitch the opening closed.

Song Riddles

Have some fun and help pass the time in the car by making up Song Riddles. These are simple short riddles you make up about family members or your child's friends, sung to the tune of "The Muffin Man." Here is an example:

Oh do you know a girl who's five?
A girl who's five, a girl who's five,
Oh do you know a girl who's five?
Who lives next door?

or

Oh do you know a big, black animal?
A big, black animal, a big, black animal?
Oh do you know a big, black animal?
Who barks very loudly?

Parent Pointer
ON THE MOVE

Take My Hand

Toddlers feel safe and secure when you are holding their hands. Whenever you are outside the security of your home, such as on the bus or subway, at the grocery store, or even at church, offer your hand to your child. The world is a much bigger place through a young child's eyes, and having your loving hand wrapped gently around his or her hand will help your child be comfortable in new surroundings.

Be careful not to force your child to hold your hand all the time if he or she doesn't want to—toddlers also enjoy their independence. Of course, there are always going to be times where it is necessary to hold your child's hand for safety reasons, such as in a crowded airport or shopping mall.

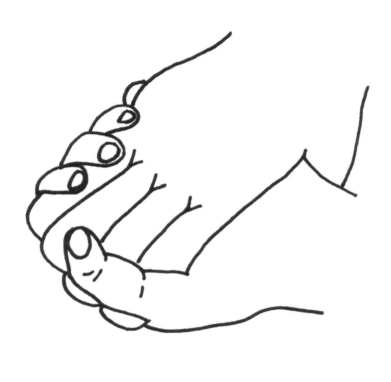

"Who Do You See?" Book

Children love to look at pictures of themselves and family members. Delight your child with such a book, patterned after the book, *Brown Bear, Brown Bear, What Do You See?* by Bill Martin. Take the "Who Do You See?" book along on trips if you will be able sit and read together. Because of the repetition of the passages on each page, your child will have the book memorized in no time but will want to read it over and over again.

Materials:

Cardboard for cover, 2 pieces, 10 by 12 inches each
Decorative self-adhesive paper
Close-up photos of family members, friends, or special people in your child's life
Poster board for the pages
Adhesive-backed plastic pocket holders in the correct size for your photos
Permanent marker
2 metal rings, 2 to 3 inches in diameter

Directions:

1. Cover the cardboard pieces with an attractive paper. Print in large letters on the front cover, "____, ____ (insert your child's name), Who Do You See?"

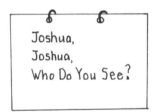

2. Cut pages from poster board, 8½ by 10 inches each, one for each picture to be used. Attach the plastic photo holder in the center of each page, using only one side of each page. Insert a picture in each holder.

3. On each page, print, "I see ____ (name of person in the photo) looking at me! Who do you see?"

4. On the very last page, insert a photo of your child and print, "I see (your child's name) looking at me."

5. Punch two holes at the top edge of each page and each cover. Assemble with two metal rings to hold the pages together.

6 While You Wait

Activities to do while waiting at places away from home, such as the doctor's office or laundry, or in quiet places such as religious services.

One of the hardest things for many parents is to deal with young children while having to wait somewhere. This is especially hard because many of the places children and parents have to wait also require children to be quiet, which is simply not a natural way for children to behave. Some waiting times are predictable, such as during religious services or at the laundry. Other times the wait may come as a surprise, when parents encounter long waits in a doctor's office or at the checkout of a grocery store.

You can help parents prepare for these waiting times by making sample activities and props ahead of time and sharing the ideas with them before the need arises. Parents will surely be appreciative of the effort you take to help them not only get through these times, but also have fun with their child while waiting.

Bag It Up

Let your child fill his or her own travel bag to take along when visiting grandparents or friends. Children are often the best judges of what they want to play with. Sometimes the bag is more fun than the contents. Toddlers just love to put things in and take things out of bags. Here is another idea that is sure to delight your child: Put a new toy in the fabric bag, close it up, and tell your child he or she can open it when you reach your destination. Curiosity will be piqued. Your child will enjoy playing with old or new toys while you get your visiting in.

Materials:
Lightweight fabric, approximately 24 inches by 10 inches
Narrow satin ribbon, approximately 10 inches long
Scissors
Sewing machine and needle and thread
Toys, either chosen by your child or a new one from you

Directions:
1. Fold the piece of fabric in half, making a 12-inch by 10-inch rectangle.
2. Sew up the sides of the rectangle on a sewing machine.
3. Sew a hem around the top of the bag.
4. With the needle and thread, tack the ribbon to the bag approximately 2 inches from the top (see illustration).
5. Fill the bag with toys, gather up the top, and tie a bow around the gathered area with the ribbon to close it.

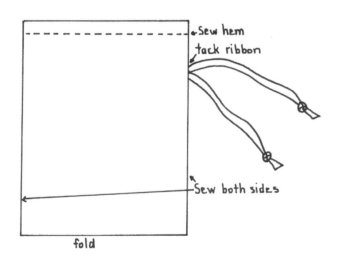

Sew hem
tack ribbon
Sew both sides
fold

A Bare-Hand Puppet

Make bare-hand puppets on you and your child. Then carry on conversations with each other through the puppets. Your child may tell the puppet some things that he or she may have a difficult time talking to you about.

To make a bare-hand puppet, first make a fist with your thumb pointing up, touching the side of your pointer finger. Tip your fist down so your thumb is horizontal. Can you see a mouth right above the thumb? Roll the tip of your thumb downwards along your pointer finger to make it look like your fist is "talking." Use a marker or pen to draw eyes, or use small sticky dots. Now you have a bare-hand puppet!

Give your bare-hand puppet a soft, silly, or squeaky voice as you chat with your child's puppet. This is sure to make waiting time more fun!

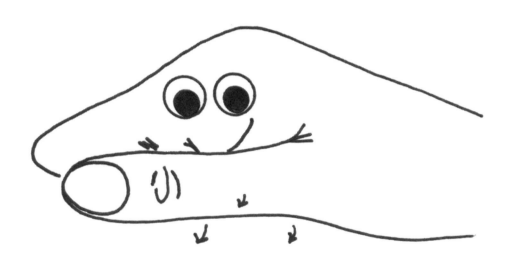

Blowing Bubbles

Bubbles are a great item to keep in your purse, backpack, or briefcase for those emergency times when you are caught waiting with nothing for your child to do. Tiny bottles of bubbles can be found in craft or "dollar" stores. These small bottles are often used at weddings. Because the wand is small, the bubbles are tiny. Children and adults find magic in tiny bubbles to track, catch, and enjoy.

If you are stuck in a traffic jam, roll the window down and you or your child can blow some bubbles. Watch them float through the air in the gentle breeze. Count to see how long before they all pop. The bubbles may even be soothing to the people in the cars around you.

While waiting for a prescription, step outside the store and blow some bubbles. Your child will also enjoy blowing bubbles while waiting at a sibling's ball game, especially when it goes into extra innings. Blowing bubbles will make the time fly by.

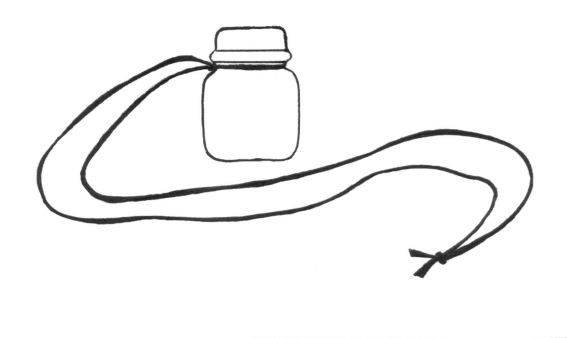

Calendar Picture Fun

Don't throw those old calendars away! The pictures are wonderful, and it is easy to cut them apart to make a book. Let your child look through the book while you are doing paperwork or studying. For times when your child is waiting withyou at the laundry or at a sibling's ball practice, take the calendar book along and talk about the pictures with your child. Initiate a story or a lively discussion about the pictures. For example, an autumn scene with children frolicking in brightly colored leaves blowing in the wind encourages discussion about the autumn weather. Show a picture of a child opening a present and ask your child to imagine what might be inside the wrapped package. Let your child do most of the talking. Interject thought-provoking questions to promote brain development and language skills.

Materials:
Pictures from old calendars
Scissors
6 page protectors, 8½ x 11 inches
   (available at office supply stores)
Three-ring binder to fit the page
protectors
Permanent marker

Directions:
1. Cut apart an old calendar with pictures that would interest your child. Ask family and friends to save them for you. Sometimes you can get free ones at a bank.
2. If necessary, cut the pictures to fit into the page protectors.
3. Slip two pictures in each page protector, back to back.
4. Place page protectors in a three-ring binder. A binder with ½-inch rings would be a good size.
5. When your child loses interest in these pictures, replace them with new ones.

Copy My Hands

"Copy My Hands" is an easy activity to engage in with your child during waiting times, such as while you are waiting for the bus or sitting in line at the drive-through bank. All you need is your hands and an imagination.

Make gestures with your hands such as waving, shaking, rolling, and so on. Encourage your child to copy you. Change the actions approximately every 10 seconds.

When you notice that your child is imitating you easily, make your gestures more complex. Some possibilities are to change the pace of the movement, the loudness of clapping, and the position of your hands in relation to your body.

Tell your child you are going to try to trick her by varying the pattern without her noticing. This challenges your child to try even harder. Reversing roles adds interest to this activity, too. Remember that the actions you do with your toddler should be much simpler than what you might do with your preschooler.

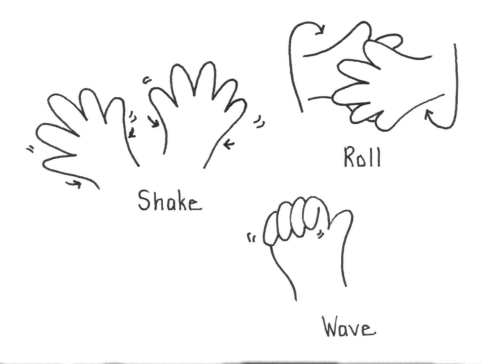

Shake

Roll

Wave

©2001 *Transition Magician for Families*; Redleaf Press, 450 North Syndicate, Suite 5, St. Paul, MN 55104, 800-423-8309

Parent Pointer
WHILE YOU WAIT

The Cutting Edge

Scissors are an intriguing tool to children. With scissors in one hand and paper in the other, your child will spend many enjoyable minutes just cutting away!

Cutting is a quiet activity, which makes it perfect for waiting times in quiet places, such as a room where a religious service or some other form of adult meeting is going on. Have you ever had a meeting scheduled, and at the last minute, your child care plan fell through? It happens! At times like this, grab the bag you filled with index cards and scissors and head on out the door, hand in hand with your child. Your child will be able to wait more patiently and quietly with this cutting activity. At the end of your meeting, pack the scissors and all the paper pieces back in a plastic bag. Take them home for a later gluing activity.

Your child will go through many stages before mastering the skill of cutting. If the child is just beginning, cut your index cards in 1-inch strips ahead of time, so that one quick snip will produce success. At the next stage, the child will be able to cut the index card with little guidance.

When your child is able to cut the index card easily, include a pencil in the bag so that you can draw a simple shape on the index card. Encourage the child to cut on the line.

A Gem in Hand

Carry a "gem" with you at all times. It's great fun for playing guessing games. Your "gem" can be a coin, marble, small rock, rubber worm, plastic bug, or anything else that you can hide in your hand.

While you are waiting with your child, take out your gem and, holding it in one hand, make fists with both hands. Let your child guess which hand the gem is in. When the child makes a guess, open the hand to see if it was correct. If not, guess again. This time it will be right! The goal, of course, is for your child to experience success.

Take a coin purse of gems with you to the doctor or dentist office. Put small numbers of gems in each hand. Have your child count the number of gems in each hand. Then add them together. This is a good activity for older preschoolers to begin simple addition. It will make the waiting time pass quickly.

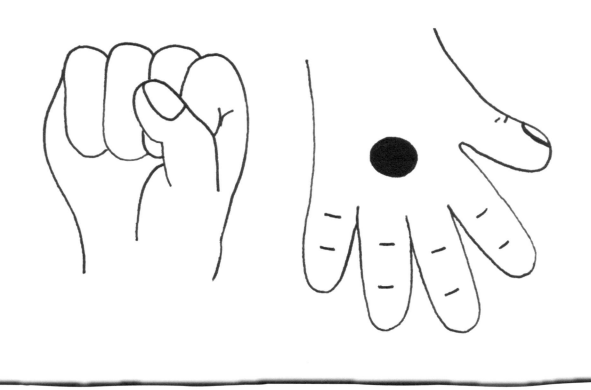

Hanky Baby

Hanky babies are delightful little "babies" made from large handkerchiefs. Your child can hold the hanky baby quietly and gently during religious services, or while you visit with friends, or anyplace where it is necessary to stay quiet and relaxed. Tell your child to take care of the baby and help it stay quiet. Your child will magically stay quiet, too!

Materials:

Inexpensive large handkerchief, approximately 16 inches square
Small amount of polyester fiberfill
⅛-inch-wide satin ribbon, approximately 20 inches long
½-inch-wide lace, approximately 6 inches long
Craft glue and scissors
Optional: Small satin rose
         Baby powder

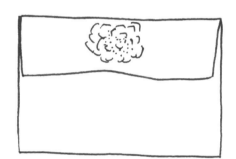

Directions:

1. Fold one side of the handkerchief about 7 inches in from the edge.
2. Place the ball of fiberfill in the middle of the fold. If desired, sprinkle a pinch of baby powder on the fiberfill to stimulate the sense of smell. Gather up the hanky around the fiberfill to become the head. Secure by tying a knot and then a bow with the satin ribbon.
3. Glue the piece of lace around the center of the head to look like the edge of a bonnet (see illustration).
4. To make arms, knot the corners of the handkerchief on either side of the head.
5. Glue the rose into the center of the bow, if desired.

How Many Fingers?

Your fingers are a great prop because they're always with you. Simply hold up some fingers and have your child count them, and tell you how many he or she sees. Then invite the child to copy you with his or her own fingers.

After you've initiated this activity for a while, let your child take a turn being the leader.

Play the "How Many Fingers" game with your child while you are waiting in line at the grocery store. This is especially easy to do if your child is facing you in a cart.

Look and See

Fill a "waiting" basket or tray with some materials so that children can "Look and See" while waiting for siblings to get home from school, while sitting on the potty-chair, or while you are talking on the telephone.

Unbreakable mirrors, kaleidoscopes, magnifying glasses, and see-through colored page protectors are good items to include in the basket or tray.

Making silly faces in the mirror is a favorite pastime for children. Your child will enjoy exploring the environment with the magnifying glass. Turning the kaleidoscope while pointing it to the light is quite magical. Looking through the colorful page protectors will make everything look red, blue, yellow, or green.

These "Look and See" items will make the waiting time pass quickly.

Parent Pointer
WHILE YOU WAIT

Object Hunt

Here is another excellent activity that supports the healthy development of the brain—and it doesn't even require any props.

Play "Object Hunt" while you are waiting in line at the grocery store, or in the drive-through at the bank. Choose something in the area and describe it to your child. See if your child can guess what object you are referring to. Use descriptive words that your child is learning, such as colors, shapes, or spatial concepts (under, over, high, low, and so on). Then reverse roles and let your child give the clues.

Passing the time with this enjoyable activity can distract your child from those not-so-nutritious foods next the to grocery store checkout. Buildings, trees, flowers, and cars can be described as you wait at the bank.

Pencil and Stencil Box

Decorate a box about the size of a pencil box (or use a large pencil pouch) and label it with your child's name. Fill the box with plain paper, colored pencils, unusual rulers, and some stencils of shapes that interest your child.

Take the Pencil and Stencil box with you to the doctor's office or other places your child must be quiet. Your child might ignore the rulers and stencils and practice freehand drawing and writing. Or your child might enjoy making shapes with the stencils and lines with the rulers. Either approach builds writing and math skills.

This is a quiet activity that will keep your child occupied for a long period of time, and it is easy to clean up.

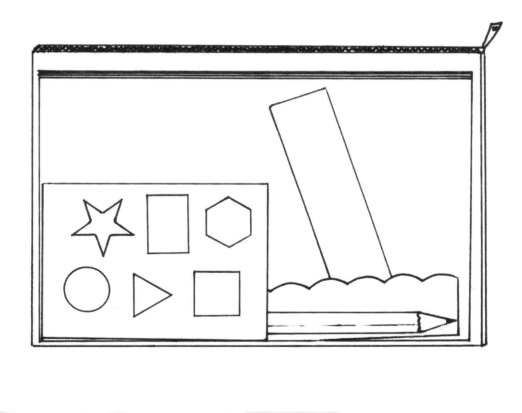

Quiet Times with the Toy Catalog

A toy catalog can be a lifesaver! All children love looking at toys and dreaming of playing with them. Keep it tucked in a special bag that only goes with your child to places where he or she needs to be quiet, such as at the dentist, doctor, or in church. The bag with the catalog could even be kept in the car, so you have it when necessary and your child is not tempted to look at it other times. This way, your child will not tire of it.

You may even get an idea of what toys your child enjoys the most. Then when it is time to shop for a special occasion, you can get the toy or toys that you know your child will play with.

You may be surprised at how long your child will spend paging through a toy catalog.

©2001 *Transition Magician for Families*; Redleaf Press, 450 North Syndicate, Suite 5, St. Paul, MN 55104, 800-423-8309

Sensory Soothers

Sensory toys such as Koosh and stress balls and small stuffed animals are great to keep with you at all times. Pull them out when your child is a little wound up or overtired and needs some soothing. Put a few in a decorative gift bag. You can even make a small fabric bag to keep them in. (Do not keep them in the car, because the heat could affect these toys.) Your child will enjoy squeezing and manipulating them. Follow the directions below to make a homemade flour-filled stress balloon.

Materials:
Large heavyweight latex balloons,
  2 per finished ball
Flour
Funnel

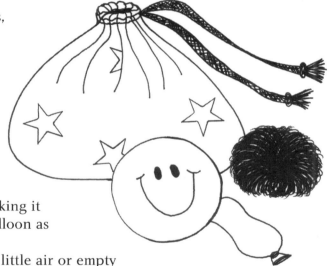

Directions:
1. Insert one balloon into another to reinforce them and prevent possible accidents. Insert a small funnel into the opening.
2. Spoon flour or salt through the funnel and into the balloon, packing it down from the outside of the balloon as you fill.
3. Double-knot the end, leaving as little air or empty space inside the balloon as possible.

Note: Do NOT use this sensory soother if your child is allergic to latex.

Spinner Story-Board

Children love to make up stories and talk about people they know. Glue pictures or photos onto a circular board to make a spinner. While you are waiting for siblings to finish practice or lessons, have your child "spin" some wonderful tales or chat fondly about grandparents, siblings, or pets with the spinner story-board. Take turns adding to the story with your child. This can be a wonderful time to build language skills, imagination, and special parent-child relationships.

Materials:
12-inch-diameter circle of
   poster board, or the card-
   board from a frozen pizza
Marker
Magazine pictures or photos
Scissors
Rubber cement
Clear Con-Tact paper
Paper fastener
Large safety or diaper pin

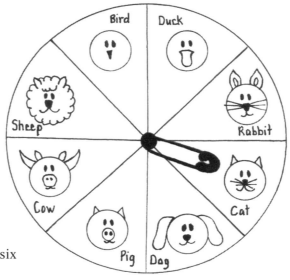

Directions:
1. Using a dark permanent marker, divide the cardboard circle into six or eight equal wedges.
2. Cut out magazine pictures of animals, foods, etc., or trim family photos to fit in the wedges.
3. Use rubber cement to adhere the pictures inside the wedges near the edge of the circle.
4. Cover the top of the circle with a self-adhesive paper such as Con-Tact.
5. To make the spinner, push the paper fastener through the loop at the end of the large safety or diaper pin.
6. Poke the points of the paper fastener through the center of the circle and bend the ends to secure it to the circle.
7. Cover the back of the circle with Con-Tact paper.

Stop-and-Go Wand

Wiggle, wiggle, wiggle, and then stop. Wiggle, wiggle, wiggle, and then stop. This easily made wand, green on one side and red on the other, will inspire this enjoyable activity. Use it to get out that excess energy that children so often have while they are waiting. Carry the wand with you in your pocket, purse, or bag of transition props. When you are stranded in rush hour traffic, or at the laundry, pull out the Stop-and-Go Wand. Chant an action that your child is developmentally capable of doing. Hold up green for a short period of time and then turn it to red and cheer joyfully when the child stops on cue. Then choose another action and start all over again.

Materials:

Poster board (the bottom of a large white gift box will do)

Red, green, and black crayons or permanent markers

Popsicle stick, tongue depressor, or paint stirrer

Glue

Scissors

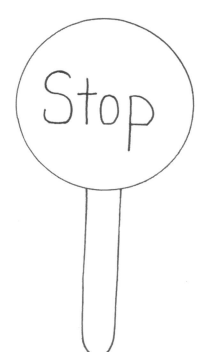

Directions:

1. Trace two circles, each approximately 5 inches in diameter, onto the poster board.

   Hint: Drawing around the top of a margarine tub or paper plate will help you make a good circle.

2. Color one side of one circle red and one side of the other circle green.

3. Write *STOP* on the red circle and *GO* on the green circle.

4. Drizzle glue on the back-side of one of the circles. Place the end of your stick 1 to 2 inches onto the glued circle to form a handle, and lay the other circle on top.

5. Press together for several minutes, and let the glue dry before using the Stop-and-Go Wand.

Parent Pointer
WHILE YOU WAIT

What's in the Feely Mitten?

"What's in the Feely Mitten?" is a fun game to play with your child during a relaxing time such as before taking a nap, or while you are waiting for supper to cook. The game requires your child to think and solve problems, which is great for brain development.

Simply insert any object that is somewhat familiar to your child into an adult-size mitten (such as a cotton garden glove). Have the child feel the outside of the mitten and guess what's inside. Examples of objects to put in the glove might be a rattle, crayon, block, rubber animal, rock, ball, spoon, milk bottle cap, etc.

Toddlers will feel the mitten for a short time and then will want to pull the object out to see what it is.

Encourage a preschooler to describe what he or she feels and guess what the object is before pulling it out. Have the child tell you if it is hard or soft, big or little, bumpy or smooth, and so on.

You can also reverse roles. Let your child find an object to put in the mitten and give you hints as to what's inside.

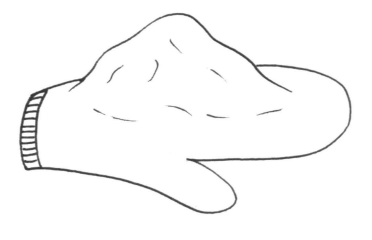

7 Transition Magician Workshops

It's the end of the day at the Almost Home Child Care Center. The children are picking up the toys and putting them back in the appropriate trays on the shelves. Miss Sideena has told the children who are waiting to be picked up by their parents that she has a special game for them when all the toys are put away. Dehlia's mom arrives to pick her up and says to Miss Sideena, "However do you get the children to pick up all the toys without fussing? Why, when I ask my children at home, I can never get them to cooperate! They dawdle around or drag out other things to play with. I usually end up yelling at them and then picking up the toys myself!" Miss Sideena acknowledges that cleanup time is often difficult for parents as well as for teachers. She thinks to herself, "This was the third parent this week who has asked about transitions. This topic would make a great workshop."

Providing parent workshops involves parents in your early childhood program. Workshops can also help parents use the tools in *Transition Magician for Families* more effectively. Workshops can provide a framework to help parents think about their daily transitions and give them an opportunity to share ideas with one another in a social setting.

This chapter gives instructions for presenting two workshops on the subject of transitions, one for parents only and the other for parents with their children, using the material in this book. The Parent Workshop gives opportunities for parents to explore their children's development and to solve their transition problems from home collaboratively with other parents. The Parent-and-Child Workshop provides an enjoyable activity for parents to do with their children, and gives parents an opportunity to identify common difficult transitions and some ideas for handling them. Both workshops have a "make and take" portion in which parents can make props and take them home along with the Parent Pointer handouts that you copy from this book. The handouts will help them remember how to use the props they have made.

The Parent Workshop includes the presentation of child development content, so it requires a bit more preparation on the part of the presenter. The Parent-and-Child Workshop is the simpler of the two workshops, because it only requires preparing materials and setting up workstations. For either workshop, feel free to make adjustments to the content and structure to meet the needs and desires of your particular group.

Parent Workshop

You will need about 2 hours and 15 minutes to present the Parent Workshop. There are three parts to the Parent Workshop. First, parents talk with one another and with the presenter about their children and their experiences with everyday routines and transitions. Next, the presenter gives a little basic information about routines and transitions in the context of child development and introduces some of the tools from *Transition Magician for Families*. Finally, parents have an opportunity to make four or five transition props to make their daily routines flow more smoothly. Parents can connect with one another while they make transition props to use at home.

Preparing for the Workshop

Before you publicize the workshop, you will have to locate a space to hold it in and decide on a time. Consider whether you will need to provide child care during the workshop (remember, this workshop is for parents only). If you decide to provide child care, you will need caregivers and a separate space for the children during the workshop. Include information about child care in your workshop promotional materials.

Read through the workshop outline. Choose five activities to highlight during the workshop, one from each transition category. Think carefully about what you have heard from parents, and choose activities that will meet the needs you hear them expressing. Use the activity chart in appendix B to select the activities. The filled-in star ★ indicates activity props that are the most appropriate for this workshop. However, the star outline ☆ indicates activities that will also work. You might also choose several other Parent Pointers to distribute, preferably ones that don't require props. In your promotional materials, you might want to highlight the kinds of activites you will emphasize in the workshop.

Once you know where and when the workshop will be held, whether there will be child care offered, and what activities you will use, you can make posters and flyers to publicize the event. Think about whether to open the workshop only to parents in your program, or to the general public in your community. This will affect how you publicize it. Be sure to include a name and phone number on the flyer, so that people will know where to call for further information and to sign up.

At least one month before the workshop, begin to publicize your *Transition Magician for Families* Parent Workshop. Announce the workshop in your newsletter; put a flyer on the parent bulletin board and send one home with the children; talk to parents as they drop off and pick up their children. If you are opening the workshop to other parents in the community, you will want to put flyers in as many places around town as possible—Laundromats, doctor and dentist offices, schools, child care centers, and family child care providers' homes. You may also want to announce it in the local or neighborhood paper. Ask parents to sign up for the workshop in advance so that you can be sure to have enough materials for everyone.

During the week before the workshop, review the selected Parent Pointer pages and prepare a sample of each prop. Make enough copies of the Parent Pointers for each parent to have a copy of each page. Also copy the first three handouts in appendix C. Gather enough materials for every participant to make one of each kind of prop. If the participant numbers are high, make this session more manageable by cutting back on the number of choices and setting up several workstations for each prop you've selected. These instructions assume that you will set up four or five workstations (one for each prop that your participants will make), which will give you room enough for twelve to fifteen people. This will spread the participants out and give them better access to the materials. You may want to make other sample transition props to show during your presentation.

You will need a flip chart for this workshop. As part of your preparations, use one sheet to make a list of the Parent Pointers you have selected, so that the parents will have a reference while they are making the props. Include the transition category of each—for example, list "Magic Pickup Lotion: Everyday Routines."

On the day of the workshop, set up one table or area for each prop, including a stack of copies of the Parent Pointer explaining the activity and giving instructions, and all of the needed materials. Post the list of Parent Pointers you are introducing in the workshop, and set up the flip chart so that you can write on it to help facilitate group discussion. If you are comfortable using an overhead projector and are certain that one will be available for your use during the workshop, you can use that instead of the flip chart and markers.

Materials for the Workshop

Flip chart and markers, or overhead projector, markers, and transparencies

Parent Quiz (appendix C), one for each participant

Activity Categories handout (appendix C), one for each participant

Parent Tips handout (appendix C), one for each participant

Parent Pointer handouts for all workshop activities, plus any others you wish to introduce

Pens or pencils and paper for each participant

Sample props

Materials to make the props you've chosen

Conducting the Workshop

Step 1 **Introduction (5 minutes)**

Begin the workshop by introducing yourself to the participants and giving them a brief idea of what you'll be doing in the workshop. For example, you might say something like the following introduction. (Be sure to put it in your own words, since you have the best idea of what will be appropriate for your audience of parents.)

"Transitions are difficult for adults and children alike, and think of all the transitions you make in one day! For some children, making the change from one activity to another is extremely difficult. The purpose of this workshop is to give you a clearer understanding of your child's development, to identify the transitions that are the most difficult for you, and to provide some transition strategies and props that you can use at home."

Ask individuals to introduce themselves before you start the warm-up activity.

Step 2 **Warm-up (20 minutes)**

Distribute the Parent Quiz, which will be a fun way to get participants to connect with each other as they recognize the familiar scenarios. Offer pens and pencils for those who need them. The point of this activity is to help participants realize that most behaviors have a cause, and that children react to what is happening in their environment. It's easier to get people to laugh by starting with questions about pet behavior than if you just jump into discussing children. (Substitute your own examples for those on the Parent Quiz if you choose.)

Ask participants to each complete the quiz on their own, which gives them time to reflect on these scenarios. When you see that some of them have finished, read the first question and ask for responses. If you are using an overhead projector, you can use a transparency of the quiz to guide the discussion.

As participants respond to the quiz, you can help make the connections between the examples on the quiz and what they experience in their own homes. For example, after question number seven is reviewed, you might make the point that waiting is difficult for three-year-olds and that they are limited in their ability to cope with waiting. As adults, we need to give a three-year-old child a prop or a plan to help them through the transition or waiting time.

Step 3 Typical Behaviors (30 minutes)

Ask participants to raise their hand if they have a two-year-old, then a three-year-old, then a four-year-old, and then a five-year-old. Ask parents to look around and notice other parents who have children the same age as theirs. Make sure everyone has something to write with, and hand out writing paper.

Ask parents to write their child's name and age on a piece of paper and list the behaviors they like best about their children. When they have done that, ask them to make a second column and list the behaviors they find frustrating or challenging about their children. You can ask them to do this on their own or to find another parent who has a child of approximately the same age and work in pairs. (Each parent should keep their own list, however.) The paper gives them something to refer to in the large-group discussion.

When most people have finished making their lists, start the large-group discussion by writing *3-year-olds* at the top of the flip chart (or on an overhead transparency) and asking them to share their lists.

This is what the list should look like:

3-Year-Olds

What Parents Like   Challenges/Frustrations

Write the responses on the paper. Do the same for the four-year-olds and the five-year-olds. Then go back to the three-year-old list and review what they have shared. As you review the list, ask them if they think a particular behavior is "normal" for a three-year-old.

As the facilitator, your role is to clarify whether the behaviors listed are typical or atypical at that developmental age. They will discover that many of the behaviors that frustrate or challenge them are really normal behaviors for that age.

Continue sharing and responding to the four-year-old and five-year-old lists in the same manner. It is very affirming for parents to have this discussion about their children's development.

When you've completed this discussion, close with a statement like this:

"It's easy to be annoyed by our children's behavior, especially when we have so many worries of our own, and we are on such tight schedules ourselves. As we found in this discussion, it helps to understand how normal most of our children's behavior is for their age. They're not trying to drive us crazy!

"Now let's look at the kinds of transitions we experience in a typical day. By looking at typical daily transitions we find at home, we may discover that we actually create some of the behavior problems—for three reasons." Turn to the flip chart and on a new sheet write down the following three reasons as you say them. (You can also prepare a sheet with these ahead of time and simply flip the flip chart to that page at this point in the workshop, or use the overhead projector.)

1. We have inappropriate expectations.

2. We overload the child with too many transitions in one day.

3. We don't give children enough time or prepare them for the transition.

Continue speaking: "We are now going to look at our expectations of our children during typical transition times during the day."

Step 4 Review Transition Categories (10 minutes)

Distribute the Transition Categories handout. Review the typical daily transitions by reading through the handout. As you describe each category, share some sample props that you have made. Talk about how the prop was made and how it can be used. Parents usually love this and will often want to take notes as you describe the props.

Step 5 Your Daily Schedule Activity (20 minutes)

Ask participants to write out a typical daily schedule, or simply ask them to record all of the activities they did yesterday from the time they got up until their child went to bed. Give them a few minutes to complete this task. Then ask them to count the number of transitions they and their child experienced in a day. Use this opportunity to discuss how difficult transitions are for most children, especially if there are many in a day.

You may say something like this, "Young children may be able to handle the first few transitions of the day without help. However, as the transitions accumulate and children become tired, they will have a harder time getting through the transition without your help. Can you think of some ways you could reduce the number of transitions?" Wait for their responses. If parents do not respond to your question, be ready with a home example of your own. Or, give an example of how you eliminated transitions in your classroom. If one person shares, others usually will.

Then ask participants to turn to a neighbor and talk about one or two of their most challenging transitions. After about three minutes, bring the group back together, and ask them to summarize their discussions as you record their comments on the flip chart or on the overhead projector. Choose two or three transitions that are mentioned the most and spend a few minutes brainstorming ideas to help ease the transition. Encourage participants to jot down ideas on the handout for future reference. Record the ideas on the flip chart and add any of your own ideas.

Conclude this part of the workshop and move into making props by saying something like, "As you can see by what we have just recorded on the chart paper, we all share common challenging transition times. By anticipating when we experience challenging transitions, we can change how we do transitions with children, and plan for them.

We can also change our reaction to them, or we can change what we do in certain situations.

"Right now you will have the opportunity to look at some of the suggestions from *Transition Magician for Families* and make some props that will help ease transitions in each of the five categories. You can choose which props you want to make based on what you feel would be most helpful for you." (Be aware that most parents will simply want to make them all, and that's fine. Just be sure you have ample materials.)

Step 6 **Transition Prop Make-and-Take (45 minutes)**

Explain that there is a workstation for each prop with all the necessary materials and copies of the Parent Pointer page with the directions. Show them where each workstation is. Ask them to choose a table where they would like to start. If there are too many participants at one table, ask for volunteers to move to another workstation and come back later. When participants complete a prop, they can select another workstation. As participants are working, encourage them to share with you and with each other how they plan to use the props. You should make yourself available to answer their questions, but you will find that they will also help each other.

Step 7 **Summary (5 minutes)**

When you see that the majority of participants are finishing up, ask them for their attention as you briefly summarize the workshop. You might say something like this:

"In this workshop, we reviewed some things about child development that reminded us that our children's behaviors are pretty normal, but that sometimes it's our expectations that are not quite appropriate. We got a better handle on the numerous transitions we experience on a daily basis with our children by looking at five different types of transition activities. We evaluated our daily schedule to discover why some transitions are more difficult than other transitions and talked about some ways of handling them. And lastly, we made some props to go with some of the strategies we chose. I hope that this time we've spent together will help you get a better handle on transitions at home!" Give them the Parent Tips handout from appendix C when they leave.

Parent-and-Child Workshop

The Parent-and-Child Workshop is an informal time for parents and their children to discuss typical transitions in the home and learn pointers for their most challenging transitions. In this workshop, five workstations will be set up for parents and their children to make transition props together. Allow one to one-and-a-half hours for this workshop, but leave it open-ended so that parents can leave when they are ready or when they have finished with their props.

Preparing for the Workshop

Two to four weeks prior to the workshop, send the Workshop Invitation (see appendix C) and the Activity Categories handout (see appendix C) to the parents. Personalize the sample invitation, or make up your own. The sample in this book says that the Transition Categories handout is included; if you do this, make sure you have plenty of extra copies the day of the workshop. Consider whether to have an activity for the children during the introductory ten minutes of the workshop, and if you decide to do this, find someone to lead this activity and plan a separate space for the children for this time.

Consult the preparation section of the Parent Workshop (pages 92–93) for more ways to publicize and prepare for a workshop.

Select the Parent Pointer ideas you will use for this workshop, one from each of the five categories, using the Activity Chart in appendix B. The activities that will work best for the Parent-Child Workshop are indicated by a filled-in star ★. These props are easily made with preschool children. Review the selected Parent Pointer pages, make a sample of each prop, and make enough copies of the selected Parent Pointer pages so that each participant will have one. Also make extra copies of the Activity Categories handout and the Parent Tips handout (both in appendix C). Based on the number of parents signed up, purchase the materials you will need.

On the day of the workshop, set up one table or area for each prop, including all the needed materials and copies of the Parent Pointer page that gives instructions for making and using that prop. Because children will be participating, the low tables in an early childhood classroom are a good choice. Prepare a sign for each category (Everyday Routines, Busy Times, Together Times, On the Move, and While You Wait), and place these signs on the appropriate tables. Also, prepare the top sheet on a flip chart with each of the five Activity Categories. Leave a space under each category to write. See the Parent Workshop instructions for ideas about using an overhead projector in place of the flip chart.

Materials

Large sheet of paper listing Activity Categories

Flip chart for taking notes during discussion

Markers

Activity Categories handout, one for each participant

Selected Parent Pointer pages, one for each participant

Parent Tips handout, one for each participant

Materials to make the props you've chosen

Category signs for tables

Conducting the Workshop

Step 1 | **Workshop Introduction (10 minutes maximum if children are present)**

Begin the workshop by introducing yourself to the participants. Ask them to introduce themselves and their children. Give them a brief idea of what you'll be doing in the workshop by saying something like the following:

"We're excited that so many of you were able to bring your children to this *Transition Magician* workshop! Based on conversations we've had with you, transitions at home (those times between activities or when children are waiting) are as challenging for you as they are for us as teachers in the classroom. We wanted to give you an opportunity to spend some quality time with your child, to learn some transition tricks, and to make some transition props to take home with you.

"Did you have a chance to read the handout about the five categories of transitions that you find at home?" Give the parents a minute to look the list over. Using the large paper with the five categories, review each one and ask them to give you some examples. Have them describe their most challenging transition in each category. Ask them which type of transition they have the most of in a day. Then explain that in this workshop they'll be making props from *Transition Magician for Families* to help them handle some of their difficult transitions, and that the instructions for each prop also explain how to use it.

Say something like, "We have selected a Parent Pointer from each category and have all the materials here for you to make the props. You and your child will work together to make the props, which you will be able to take with you along with the Parent Pointers."

Step 2 | **Parent-Child Make-and-Take Activity (30-45 minutes)**

Explain how the workstations are set up and labeled. Explain to the participants that they can make all the items or do the ones of their choice, but that they should gauge the number by the child's participation and interest. Suggest that they start with the Parent Pointers that they think will help them the most and then move on to others. They should also involve their child in this selection. Encourage parents and children to interact during the activity. Be available if parents need assistance. (You may want to preview how to make each prop before they begin.) Remind parents that this time is open-ended and that you will not be offended if they or their children need to leave before finishing their props.

Step 3 | **Workshop Summary**

When you notice that most participants have finished making the props, conclude the workshop by calling for the parents' attention and saying something like this:

"We hope you have enjoyed this time with your child. The Parent Pointers in *Transition Magician for Families* are designed to promote quality time with your child. We are also sending with you a Parent Tips handout that will give you additional ideas to make transitions at home more manageable." (Give them the handout as they leave.)

Appendix A: Resources

Recommended books on brain development:

Diamond, Marian Cleeves, and Janet L. Hopson. *Magic trees of the mind: How to nurture your child's intelligence, creativity, and healthy emotions from birth through adolescence.* New York: Penguin Putnam, 1998.

Gopnik, Alison, Andrew N. Meltzoff, and Patricia K. Kuhl. *The scientist in the crib: Minds, brains, and how children learn.* New York: William Morrow, 1999.

Jensen, Eric. *Teaching with the brain in mind.* Alexandria, Va.: Association for Supervision and Curriculum Development, 1998.

Ramey, Craig T., and Sharon L. Ramey. *Right from birth: Building your child's foundation for life.* New York: Goddard Press, 1999.

Shore, Rima. *Rethinking the brain: New insights into early development.* New York: Families and Work Institute, 1997.

Siegel, Daniel J. *The developing mind: Toward a neurobiology of interpersonal experience.* New York: Guilford Press, 1999.

Other *Transition Magician* books:

Larson, Nola, Mary Henthorne, and Barbara Plum. *Transition magician: Guiding young children in early childhood classrooms.* St. Paul: Redleaf Press, 1994.

Henthorne, Mary, Nola Larson, and Ruth Chvojicek. *Transition magician 2: More strategies for guiding young children in early childhood programs.* St. Paul: Redleaf Press, 2000.

Appendix B: Workshop Activity Lists

Everyday Routines
Job and Joy Jars p.7 ★
Let Me Hand it to You p.8 ☆
Point the Way p.15 ★
Puppet Patrol p.16 ★
Quiet as a Mouse p.17 ☆

Busy Times Activities
Bat the Ball p.23 ☆
A Circle of Match-Ups p.28 ★
Pizza Box Felt Board p.35 ☆
Puzzle Put-Togethers p.37 ☆
Sound Jars p.38 ★

Together Times
Bottle of Names p.45 ☆
Card with Peek Holes p.48 ☆
Dots p.50 ☆
Favorite Things to Do p.52 ★
Message In an Egg p.54 ☆
Pinhole Wand p.56 ☆
Shaker Bottles p.57 ★
Super Streamers p.58 ☆

On the Move
Color Cards p.59 ☆
Love Tickets p.64 ☆
Magnetic Fingertips p.66 ☆
Pillow Pleasantries p.68 ★

While You Wait
A Bare-Hand Puppet p.75 ★
Calendar-Picture Fun p.77 ☆
Hanky Baby p.81 ☆
Spinner Story-Board p.88 ★
Stop-and-Go Wand p.89 ☆

★—Indicates Parent-and-Child
   Workshop Activities

☆—Indicates Parent Workshop
   Activities (any of the Parent-
   and-Child Workshop Activities
   will work for the Parent workshop)

Appendix C:
Handouts and Examples

Tips for Parents

Six ways to help your child through transitions and routines

1 **Think about your child's day.** How many transitions are there? It might be helpful to actually write out a schedule from the time he or she gets up in the morning until bedtime at night. Are some times harder than others? Could some transitions be eliminated? For example, instead of picking your child up from school or child care and then stopping at the grocery store on the way home, you might consider stopping at the store before picking up your child. This way your child can go directly from school to home. Much less stress! Also, if your child moves from one early childhood program to another during the day (for example, from preschool or Head Start to child care), you might look for a facility that has both options in one setting so that your child can stay in one place during the day.

2 **Be prepared.** Carry a bag of tricks, just as a teacher does in the classroom. Fill it with a few toys, props, and gadgets that will pass the time quickly, and change them every so often. Stick a few things in your pocket, your purse, or the glove compartment of your car so that you are prepared at all times.

3 **Create a consistent routine for your child.** Knowing what to expect every day and sticking to a schedule is much easier on children (and parents too!). Take photos of your child at various times throughout the day to create a pictorial schedule. This visual cue helps children understand the passing of time. When changes of schedule arise, talk about them in advance if possible so that your child isn't taken by surprise.

4 Create a collection of activities that you can pull out while you are busy with things like housework, schoolwork, or phone calls. Keep these activities on a special shelf or in a cupboard so that your child knows they can only be played with when you get them out. Keeping them separate from everyday toys helps these special activities remain interesting to your child.

5 Turn off the television and play with your child. Between supper and bedtime, or on rainy afternoons, don't just pop a video into the VCR. Put on some music and dance together, look at photo albums and tell stories about the people in the photos, or play a simple matching game together. Research on brain development tells us that music, movement, and verbal interaction actually help a child grow smarter. Ask your child's teacher for more "healthy brain" activities.

6 Don't just try to "survive" these sometimes-stressful times with your child. Turning them into fun, magical times will create wonderful memories for both of you. For example, singing together into a pretend microphone during a long car trip can instantly transform a trying situation into a treasured memory. Have fun, and enjoy your wonderful child!

Parent Quiz

1. What happens to most dogs when meat is eaten in front of them?

    a. They do a little dance.

    b. They lie down and go to sleep.

    c. They drool.

    d. They ignore you.

2. You leave your new puppy in the house alone for 15 minutes while you run to the store. While you are gone, the puppy:

    a. Has chewed your brand-new tennis shoes.

    b. Has eaten your dinner off the counter.

    c. Has chewed the arm off the couch.

    d. All of the above.

3. What does the average teenager do when you announce it's time to clean his or her room?

    a. Thanks you for the opportunity to keep your home clean.

    b. Gets up early and cleans the entire house before you are awake.

    c. No need to clean—his or her room is always spotless.

    d. Cleans the room only after you threaten to take away TV for a month.

4. What does your five-year-old do when bedtime is announced?

    a. She runs around the house pulling out every toy she owns.

    b. She suddenly becomes deaf.

    c. She goes to bed quietly and immediately.

    d. Any or all of the above.

5. How long does the average four-year-old sit quietly and calmly in religious services?

   a. The entire service.

   b. 30 minutes.

   c. 3-5 minutes.

   d. 15 minutes.

6. What does your preschooler do when you all wake up late and have only 15 minutes to get ready for work and school?

   a. Either sits and watches TV or plays in his or her pajamas, refusing to get dressed.

   b. Spills breakfast cereal all over the floor.

   c. Tells you as you are running out the door that he or she needs money and a sack lunch for a field trip at school.

   d. All of the above.

7. What is a three-year-old most likely to do while waiting (for a long time) in a doctor's office?

   a. Run circles around the chairs in the waiting room.

   b. Ask 100-plus questions.

   c. Fall asleep two minutes before the nurse announces it's finally your turn.

   d. All of the above.

8. You arrive home from work later than usual because you had to stop at the grocery store and the gas station on the way home. Now you discover you forgot to take the hamburger out of the freezer earlier to thaw for supper. Your preschooler is starving.

   He or she:

   a. Sits quietly reading a book.

   b. Whines and cries begging for food.

   c. Quietly sits coloring while you cook.

   d. Says that's okay; he or she knows you're busy and can wait as long as necessary for dinner.

Activity Categories

Everyday Routines

Activities to help a parent guide a child smoothly through routines at home, such as getting ready to leave the house in the morning, picking up toys, or getting ready for bed.

Busy Times

Special activities for a child to do on his or her own while the parent is busy with household routines and responsibilities, such as preparing a meal, talking on the telephone, cleaning the house, or studying.

Together Times

Quality activities for parent and child to do together in the midst of daily routines.

On the Move

Activities for children to do while traveling, both on the everyday trip to school or child care, and on longer trips.

While You Wait

Activities to do while waiting at places away from home, such as at the doctor's office or at the laundry, or while the child waits quietly during an adult meeting.

Workshop Invitation

(Date)

Dear Parents,

We have had many requests from parents to have a workshop that you and your child can attend together. Many of you have asked us for ideas about transition activities at home. For example, "What do I do with my children as we are driving?" or "What can I do to get my child settled down for bed?" You and your child are invited to attend the Transition Workshop to get some ideas on how to handle these challenging times. The workshop will be held on _____ at _____. The workshop is open-ended, which means you can stay as long as you wish with your child.

We are sending you a description of five transition categories to read before the workshop. You might like to think about the categories that are the most challenging for you and your child. At this workshop, we will talk about transitions at home, and you and your child will make props that will help make these transitions smoother and actually fun.

Please register for this workshop on the sign-up sheet on the Parent Bulletin Board (or designated location).

We hope to see you there!

Sincerely,

Other Resources from Redleaf Press

Transition Magician: Strategies for Guiding Young Children in Early Childhood Programs
By Nola Larson, Mary Henthorne, & Barbara Plum
More than 200 original learning activities weave smoothness into activity changes.

Transition Magician 2: More Strategies for Guiding Young Children in Early Childhood Programs
By Mary Henthorne, Nola Larson, & Ruth Chvojicek
Offers over 200 original learning activities, more than 50 props and games, and adaptations for toddlers and for children with special needs.

So This Is Normal Too? Teachers and Parents Working Out Developmental Issues in Young Children
By Deborah Hewitt
Makes the challenging behaviors of children a vehicle for cooperation among adults and stepping stones to learning for children.

Practical Solutions to Practically Every Problem: The Early Childhood Teacher's Manual
By Steffen Saifer
Over 300 proven developmentally appropriate solutions for all kinds of classroom problems.

Big as Life: The Everyday Inclusive Curriculum, Volumes 1 & 2
By Stacey York
From the author of *Roots and Wings,* these two curriculum books explore the environment of a child's life and the connections that make life meaningful.

The Kindness Curriculum: Introducing Young Children to Loving Values
By Judith Anne Rice
Create opportunities for kids to practice kindness, empathy, conflict resolution, and respect.

Making It Better: Activities for Children Living in a Stressful World
By Barbara Oehlberg
Offers bold new information and activities to engage children in self-healing and empowerment.

Infant and Toddler Experiences
By Fran Hast & Ann Hollyfield
Filled with experiences—not activities—that promote the healthiest development in infants and toddlers.

800-423-8309
www.redleafpress.org